DIVORCED
DAD

Kids are Forever, Wives are Not

L.J. Burke

DIVORCED DAD

Kids are forever, Wives are not

L.J. Burke

TABLE OF CONTENTS

Introduction

Thank you for buying my book "Divorced Dad" Kids are forever, wives are not. Please don't be confused by the title. I am a proponent of marriage and everything it stands for. I believe however sometimes things don't go as planned and you will find yourself in divorce court. It means you are breaking up with your spouse, not your kids. They are *the* most important thing to consider while going through a divorce.

I wrote this book looking back at my divorce with clarity seeing what I did wrong and what I did right during this tough time. It is my sincere hope that if you are contemplating, going through or have gone through a divorce, this book will help you through this very tough time. In this book, I have condensed the lessons I have learned about divorce and relationships before, during and after my divorce. I will tell you what I did wrong and what I did right during this life changing time of my life.

After my wife had moved out and I was no longer enjoying a "duel income" and started paying an exorbitant amount of child support I was staring foreclosure of my house, bankruptcy, and a very bitter custody/placement battle straight in the eyes. This was all drawn out for years in a bitter court battle. The woman that I used to call my wife lied, stole from me, manipulated our children against me and committed perjury in court, in an attempt to win the battle.

I'm not a Psychologist, Psychiatrist, lawyer or a therapist. I'm just a regular guy who survived a terrible divorce and the lessons it taught me. This book is not meant to be legal or mental health advice in any way. So please don't sue me. I'm just a regular guy with two kids who found himself in a horrible divorce that nearly tore my kids and me apart at the seams.

I live in Wisconsin, and this is a "no fault" state when it comes to divorce. You don't have to prove who was to blame for the divorce. Everything is assumed to be a 50/50 split when you divorce. Things like property, assets, debt, and placement and custody. In Wisconsin, Placement is where and whom the children live with. Custody is making decisions regarding them. Examples are going into the military, getting a driver's license or any other big decisions.

I truly appreciate you taking the time to read my work. If you enjoyed this book, please consider leaving a favorable review wherever you bought this book. Also, if you could tell your friends and family about my books, I would truly appreciate it. Thank you.

CHAPTER ONE

Listen to Your Gut

I know I'm not alone in the fact that I went through a horrendous divorce. There are plenty of folks that have gone through or are going through much worse than what happened to me. I sincerely hope, you the reader, get something out of my book that will help you out during this awful event in people's lives.

My name is Liam Burke. When my divorce kicked off, I was in my mid 40's, married for a little over 20 years and had two boys that I love dearly. I will try to protect their privacy as much as possible in this book. So if you think I'm not being specific enough when it comes to my kids, that's why. I worked nights as a Police Sergeant in a big city and loved my job. I work during the day now in a slower part of town and have learned to appreciate all that it has to offer.

Both of my parents are Irish immigrants, and I was raised in a very strict Irish Catholic house. They got married to each other when they were about 18 years of age and were devout Catholics. This meant my brother and I had to be devout Catholics also. Going to mass every Sunday and feeling guilty about everything was par for our course. Not to mention that divorce is a mortal sin and not an option. No matter what the circumstances are. As you can guess, it was very tough on my folks also. My mother is convinced I bought a one-way ticket to hell by getting divorced.

I met my future wife while in college when I was about 22 years of age. Sam was two years younger than me and dropped out of college shortly after we started dating. We got engaged after about nine months of dating. Looking back, we were both very young, and that probably wasn't the most mature thing to do. I graduated from college about a year later, and we got married about five months after that. I wished we would have lived together first for a while. Both of our parents were Catholic, so that was out of the question. We tried too hard to make them happy, instead of working on our relationship and getting to know each other better. I think you are in the "honeymoon" stage of a relationship for the first six months to a year. I believe you don't see each other's faults, and you tend to put your partner on a pedestal. Living together is a viable option, as long as you don't make it an excuse not to commit to each other. I also believe that you should be married when you start having kids. I'm sure that will piss off some folks, but that is how I feel. Of course, there are awesome folks that raise great kids in 'non-traditional' households. I can't help how I feel and how I was raised.

We moved to a bigger city in Wisconsin and Sam attended a technical college and received her associates degree. We both worked crazy hours and really didn't see each other that much. We never put time aside for just "us" and we definitely didn't nurture our relationship. We both assumed everything would be ok when we stopped working crazy hours and started a family. We were both wrong.

She worked as a cook in restaurants, and I worked in restaurants as a manager. That meant I was the cook, the dishwasher, the host and whatever else that was needed when somebody didn't show up for work; which was usually every night that I worked. I then sold cars and bartended for about four years before I got my chance to be a big city cop. During this time, we really didn't see each other all that much, and we just went through the motions of being married. Sam and I wanted a family, but we wanted to own a home, and I had to have a job that had a good paycheck and good health insurance. Sam made more money than me during this time, and she reminded me of this fact on a regular basis. She complained endlessly about my jobs. It was never enough money or whatever else she found wrong with my jobs. This, of course, pissed me off since I was testing for different police and fire departments and working about 60 hours a week. This and other things started to build resentment between the both of us.

Our relationship was not a very loving one, and we fought often. Sam thought that once I got a job as a police officer, all of our problems would disappear. We should have worked on our relationship and examined why things were not going so great. Instead of hoping everything would be great when I was making good money, and we could buy a house and start having kids. I should have insisted that we work on our relationship instead of ignoring that nagging feeling in my gut of doom and hoping everything would 'work out'.

Always listen to your gut, it's usually right.

CHAPTER TWO

The Perfect Storm

So the day came, and I got accepted into the police academy in the biggest city in Wisconsin. It was six months of a boot camp-like experience. I was busy running, marching, shooting and getting my head stuffed with city ordinances and state statues   Sam was busy packing up our house and quitting her job. She saw this as our golden opportunity to finally have some stability and start a family. It should have been just that, an ***opportunity***.

On our first day of the academy, we had one of many guest speakers address our class. He stood up at the podium and informed us how our lives were going to change. He also informed us of the very grave divorce statistics for police officers. He informed us that because of our new profession, there was about an 80% chance we would wind up in divorce court. Those were certainly not great odds, and I couldn't help think this could wind up me in a few years; especially since we already were having some trouble with our marriage. Later that night I informed Sam of this grim divorce statistic, and all she could talk about was how much money I would be making and us finally owning a home.

Sam completely ignored these grim statistics, and I let her. Sam was blinded with the ideas of money and stability, not that these things are bad but like everything else in life there is a price tag. She did not take into consideration the price both of us would pay for the "American dream." My new job would include an enormous amount of stress and lack of sleep due to working long hours at night; I should have pushed the issue and opened up a dialogue about this. I just didn't want to fight. I was very good at conflict avoidance.

While I was in the academy, we moved into our first home. It was a modest ranch style house in a great neighborhood. I absolutely loved it, and Sam thought of it as a "nice starter house."

Time passed by, and I made it through the academy. Around the same time, Sam found a job in food service working Monday through Friday with weekends off during day shift hours. She even had summers off. I was assigned to the busiest and most dangerous part of the city working midnight to eight in the morning. This meant working weekends and most holidays. Workdays were usually more than eight hours. My shifts often turned into 10, 12, 16 or more hours. It was non-stop action with, shootings, stabbings, robberies and lots of chasing bad guys. I absolutely loved it! But it started taking a toll on my body. I was exhausted all the time and Sam showed no empathy or sympathy for me. I was on the nightly news many times at some big crime scene. Sam was indifferent to all of this, and she would get infuriated and defensive when one of her friends called after seeing the news making sure I was ok. "I have a tough job too!" I would hear on a regular basis. She is one of the most competitive persons I have ever known. I would try to reassure her and tell her that her job was important also, but mine had a lot more danger and responsibility. I would use the phrase, "It's not a competition, it's ok if people are worried about me." She would just grimace and change the subject. She had absolutely no empathy or sympathy for me and the very stressful job I had.

It was at this moment in our relationship that we should have sought professional help. Neither of us even brought up the topic. The department really didn't do a whole lot back then to support the cops emotionally. I couldn't talk to my traditional parents; they would just worry about my soul and me burning in hell. I did talk to my friends about this stuff over beers, but they all had their problems too. I certainly didn't want to seem like some kind of wimp, especially around my police circle of friends.

This was a perfect storm for serious problems, and our marriage was in jeopardy, even if we didn't fully realize it at that time.

CHAPTER THREE

In-laws, cancer, financial crisis and marriage counseling

Time went on, and Sam gave birth to two boys in five years. I couldn't have been happier about that. They were happy and healthy and continue to be the apple of my eye. She continued to work full-time, and I stayed on the late shift.

I attempted to watch our first child when I got home from work. Sam thought it would be "no problem" for me to work at night and watch our son during the day while she worked. It sounded good in theory, but trying to function on very little sleep didn't work out so great for me. I would work all night and pick up our son at the sitter around eight, or whenever I got off work. I would then watch him until Sam came home from work in the evening. As you might have guessed, this just didn't work. I was exhausted all the time and my work suffered. Being a cop in the most dangerous part of town with little to no sleep at night was just plain stupid. It put my comrade's lives and mine in danger.

Sam had zero empathy for me staying up all day after working all night. My resentment towards her was growing like the weeds in our neglected backyard. We started to fight about almost everything. I would jump for joy inside if she was going to go out of town, or just be away from me for a little bit. "This is not how married folks should act." I thought to myself many times.

Late shift continued to kick my ass, and it was taking a toll. I did enjoy my job and I could have transferred to the early shift, which would have meant I would have worked four until midnight. Unfortunately, that would also mean I wouldn't see my kids or Sam all that much. I wanted to be a good father and husband so that shift wouldn't have worked. So I was destined to be a vampire for many years to come.

After about a year in purgatory, Sam and I agreed it was time to put our son in daycare. This was a bitter pill to swallow to be sure. I felt so guilty like I was the worlds worse Dad. I thought I should have been stronger, but I couldn't keep this lifestyle of no sleep and very little help or support from Sam up much longer. I didn't want our son being raised by strangers, but I knew we couldn't go on like this. Sam wanted to continue to work full-time, and there was no stopping her. She had to feel "important" in her mind. She couldn't compete for attention with me if she were just a "stay at home Mom." Daycare was very expensive, and most of what Sam made went to that bill every month.

We should have worked together as a team, not in some weird *competition* for attention. I honestly didn't want all the questions and comments I would get bombarded with at every one of Sam's family functions or gatherings. There has to be communication between couples. Partners should have each other's backs. I should have put on the brakes and worked all of this out with Sam. Again, I was completely exhausted both physically and emotionally and avoided the fighting. I should have pushed through it and came to some agreement with Sam.

This was the time our money problems started to kick off. We were now faced with very large daycare bills not to mention all the other expenses of children. We fell into the credit card abyss and never recovered. Again, this would have been a good time to sit down and talk about our finances and come to an agreement. Instead, we both ignored the elephant in the room, as it slowly sat on the both of us and started to suffocate us financially. We should have come up with a plan together. Even if it meant we would do without some creature comforts. But that never happened.

The resentment and ill feelings toward one another continued to build. One of the biggest stressors on or marriage was my mother-in-law. Sybil was her name, and she was mentally ill. A doctor never officially diagnosed her, but everybody knew she was, for lack of better words, nuts. When she had that "I'm going to go crazy" look on her face, you knew things weren't going to turn out ok. Of course I expected her to take Sam's side in any disagreement, but she would take it way overboard. They would feed off of each other. I believe they invented the original "Pity Party." When there was any kind of conflict between Sam and myself, she would put her head down and then abruptly snap it back up and blurt out some kind of inappropriate remarks. There is a time and place for in-law interjection. She had no filter in her brain for that. It didn't matter if we were in public or private.

Sam never stood up for me when her mother was going for my jugular. Even when she knew Sybil was dead wrong. When you're married you should look out for each other and stand up for each other. This means interjecting politely or maybe not so politely when there are over zealous parents that are trying to 'help.' This was a problem of mammoth proportions for us, and we did not resolve it.

Sybil's outburst became much worse when the divorce kicked off. She didn't realize this, but her lack of self-control actually helped me out a great deal during my divorce. She and Sam were caught in some big lies that absolutely destroyed all credibility they had.

When you are going through a divorce, and there are outside entities that are evaluating how good of a parent you are, this is not the time for you and your crazy mother to make big scenes or accuse your soon to be ex-spouse of things that just aren't true. *Especially* in front of your kids! Those kinds of outbursts really hurt your kids.

So I have to thank Sybil. It was because of her inability to control herself in public and crazy lies that I actually prevailed in my quest for 50 / 50 placement and custody of my kids. Way to go Sybil!

Time marched on and the kids got bigger, the bills got larger and so did our relationship problems. Sure, there were some good times, but there were now more bad times than good. The big yelling matches had turned into stone silence. This, of course, was a big sign that the end was nearing.

I had attempted marriage counseling a couple of years after our first son was born. Sam wasn't open to it at all. I told her I would go by myself, but she just ignored me when I spoke of it. I went to about three sessions by myself. I thought you had to go to marriage counseling with your spouse, but I was wrong. If your spouse isn't open to the idea of counseling, go by yourself. Really, it's ok. The counselor was a Psychiatrist and I had never been to a "shrink" before. She specialized in marital problems, and she had a pretty big fan base with cops and firefighters. So I thought to myself, "It can't hurt." I actually enjoyed our time together and after a couple of sessions she told me I shouldn't be married to Sam. "What?" I thought these doctors fixed these kinds of problems. Perhaps they do sometimes, but there are situations where you are better off parting ways. She was there to help me cope with all of it.

My therapist told me it was time to bring Sam into this mix, and I agreed. I presented the idea to her and she, again, would ignore me when I would bring the topic up.

Instead of pushing the issue or being more creative, I stopped going to the shrink. I do regret that very much.

I remember sitting across from the doctor and her telling me, "You and Sam may not be husband and wife, but you will be Dad and Mom forever for your kids. You're going to have to see her at all kinds of significant events in their lives. You're going to have to figure a way out to get along for your kids' sake during these times."

No truer words could have been spoken. I still think of that afternoon in her office and what she said to this day.

I'm a big believer in marriage counseling. You have to go into it with realistic expectations, though. A lot of times they don't "fix" the "unfixable." Sometimes it just plain doesn't work out. But, it is good to get some help with dealing with what might become an inevitable divorce.

About five years after my second son was born I received some earthshaking news from my doctor after a surgical procedure. I had cancer. I won't go into the gory particulars about this, but as you can imagine this news had me shaken to the core. I knew I was going to go through this by myself.

I endured three surgeries in four months. I was in a lot of pain and not in the best of moods. Sam didn't go to the first surgery, because, as she put it, she was just too busy at work. After that, I didn't want her near me for the next couple, and she didn't want to be there anyway. It took about six months to get totally well with a lot of support from family and friends, not my wife.

This would have been a good time to come together as a couple and get through this. We did the opposite, I had almost no support from her, and she couldn't stand it when somebody in our families or friends would show any kind of concern or comfort toward me.

My resentment towards Sam was growing very quickly. Our financial situation was getting worse as time went on. There were private schools, a giant second mortgage, club sports and nice cars. This also meant our credit card balances were completely out of control. The financial noose was getting tighter around our necks, and we didn't do anything together to take care of it.

Just like the cancer situation, this would have been a good time to work together as a team. If the boat is sinking, hold on to your partner and make it through. Don't push each other away and watch each other drown.

CHAPTER FOUR

How to Tell Your Spouse You Want a Divorce and Breaking the News to Your Kids

It was a beautiful spring day; Sam and I were driving down the road in her convertible. The wind and sun were in our faces. This was not the annoying blinding sun; instead, it was a warming comforting sun. This should have been an incredible moment for us together. Unfortunately for us, we were on our way to the lawyer's office that we were going to use to help us declare bankruptcy. We didn't say a word to each other most of the way. When we were about 5 minutes away from his office, I blurted out, "This would go much better if we filed separately." Sam stared straight ahead and said, "Do you want a divorce?" I told her, "yes" and we didn't say a word to each other until we got to the attorney's office.

We wound up in the lawyers conference room and he explained all the grisly details of bankruptcy. I asked him if it would be better for both of us if we filed separately and he said yes. He informed us that in order to do that we would have to be divorced, or be going through a divorce. I told him that was our intent. We finished at his office and drove home without saying a word to each other.

Looking back, this only showed how dysfunctional our relationship was. I just suggested that we dissolve a 20 plus year marriage for the first time, and that didn't spark any conversation. I thought for sure we would be up all night discussing this. If I ever had any doubts about our relationship being dead, this confirmed it. A couple of weeks went by and it was business as usual for us. We never talked about breaking up and really didn't talk about us heading to bankruptcy court.

It was a Saturday morning, and I went to bed about six after working a tough night shift. Sam came into our bedroom at about nine and woke me up. "I have something to tell you," she said in a soft tone. She went on to explain that she had been talking to divorce lawyers for some time and filed for divorce last Thursday. She also went on to say that she had a divorce attorney ten years prior to this, but chickened out at the last minute. She smiled at me and said, "I'll let you get back to sleep now" and she left the room closing the door behind her.

Is this some kind of crazy dream? Did this just happen? I thought to myself it utter disbelief.

This would have been a good time to talk. I strongly suggest that when you are going to break the big news to your spouse, you do it right. I know what you're thinking. What about you blurting out you wanted a divorce while driving to the bankruptcy lawyer's office? That was stupid of me. But, it should have opened up a conversation about the status of our relationship. Remember, how you tell your spouse that you want a divorce will be remembered forever.

Here are some suggestions on how to tell your spouse you want a divorce the right way;

-Make sure you're in a quiet, private place free from distractions. This might take a little planning, but you certainly don't want to be interrupted during this conversation.

-Pick a time when you are both well rested. It's going to be emotional enough, running on little sleep will just amp up the emotions.

-Be SOBER! A drunken conversation about divorce usually results in a fight about divorce. Nothing gets resolved at 2:00 a.m. after a night of drinking.

-Don't be an asshole or a bitch! You will gain nothing from name calling or being rude. Remember this moment will be remembered forever. Family, friends and, unfortunately, your kids will eventually find out how all of this went down.

-Have an exit strategy. You're telling your spouse that you no longer want to be married to them; this means somebody will have to leave. You should have that planned out before this conversation. One of you might have to leave quicker than you were thinking, so have an idea where you will live or where your partner can go.

- Be compassionate, but don't give the wrong idea to your spouse. You don't have to be cold as ice, but don't go overboard with the touching or hugging. Your mind is made up and you don't want to be married to this person anymore. Don't muddy up the waters with anything that could be misconstrued as any kind of romantic gesture.

This is a time to be very clear about your intentions. Don't say one thing and do another.

We didn't talk about the divorce the rest of the day. We both did a good job of avoiding each other the rest of the day. I knew it was coming, but I still felt numb. The next few weeks Sam brought up that she would be moving to a neighboring suburb as soon as possible. I had to live in the city as a condition of my employment, and Sam was all too happy to leave our house. Sam didn't give a specific timetable. I wish she had secured a place to live and a moving day. It is very stressful living in the same house as somebody that doesn't want to be married to you anymore.

The toughest part of my divorce was telling the kids that their Mom and Dad weren't going to be together anymore. I avoided this inevitable conversation for weeks. Sam was pushing hard to break the news. She was correct, you don't want them finding out through friends or other family members. You owe it to them to break the news as soon as possible.

It was a nice Saturday morning, and Sam woke me up after I had been sleeping for about a couple of hours. I wasn't mad at her this time. We had to tell the kids. So I dragged my ass out into the kitchen and sat at the table with the kids. Sam paced around the kitchen like a lion who was stalking her prey.

Sam started the conversation with, "Kids, we have to tell you something." She stopped and looked at me for what felt like an eternity. "OK, I guess I will do the dirty work," I thought to myself. Now I was wide-awake. "There's no easy way to say this, kids, but your mother and I are getting a divorce." Both kids smiled at me and told us that they already knew. They both said they heard Sam having conversations with her divorce lawyer. (Remember, kids are incredible in hearing when they want to.) I went on and told them that we would still be a family; only it will be different now. I wanted to stress how we both loved them, and nobody was going to get abandoned.

I asked if they had any questions and they both said no. They both got up from the table and went on with their regular routines. I wasn't sure what to think of this. My stomach was still in a knot, and I felt horrible. Sam just continued to pace and really didn't say all that much.

I don't think there is a perfect way to tell your kids that you're getting divorced. There are so many factors; age, maturity, any kind of special problems with physical or mental health. There is no easy way to do this. I believe honesty is the most important thing to keep in mind. Don't give your kids any false sense of hope that you will not break up. There are way too many Disney movies where divorced couples wind up back together in some magical zany way. Shame on you Disney!

If you really have no idea how to break the news to your kids, I would suggest you go to a family therapist. Also, it would probably be a good idea for the kids to see a therapist at this very confusing and often difficult time. Make sure you reassure your kids often that you both still love them very much and will do everything in your power to make this process as painless as possible. Do this often through the divorce process. Protecting your kids is priority one!

CHAPTER FIVE

Time to Get a Good Lawyer

Some folks who break up do so amicably and are able to get away with using one lawyer or hire a professional mediator. Hurray for you if that's the case! If you're going to go that route, you have to have all or most of the particulars regarding the division of assets, and debt, placement of children and any other issues worked out before you step foot in their offices. I believe that is a rare occasion to be sure. It's a good idea to still get a lawyer that you trust to check out whatever deal you struck with your ex. These decisions will affect you for many years.

When Sam dropped the divorce bomb on me, I thought to myself, "I'm going to need a good lawyer." I started to talk to some folks on the job that either went through horrible divorces or knew somebody that went through a terrible divorce and were happy with their lawyers. Unfortunately, in my line of work, there were plenty of folks to talk to. One of my former bosses went through a terrible divorce complete with a crazy ex-wife that would set his clothes on fire and throw them out the window of their house as a weekly event. He actually did ok and was happy with his lawyer. I expected the worse from Sam, so that was the first lawyer I went to. I also went on-line and checked him out. He had many positive reviews, and that reassured me.

You may not know a bunch of folks that have gone through divorces. So, there are varieties of web sites that specialize in finding lawyers that can be helpful to you in your search. AVVO is a national search engine for finding lawyers and has funny commercials. You can also look at message boards online with reviews and check with the bar association in your state to see if there are complaints about certain lawyers.

It is a good idea to retain a lawyer that specializes in divorce law in your area. They know the judges, court commissioners and should be educating themselves on a regular basis on any changes in divorce law. They can help you navigate through the legal minefield that you will be tiptoeing through. They usually fall under the umbrella of practicing "Family Law".

Try to avoid using lawyers that are "family friends" that usually don't practice divorce law. Your friend that spends most of his or her time practicing immigration law may not be the best fit for this situation. They may have best intentions and save you some money up front, but it might cost you a lot of money in the long run. Would you hire a hand surgeon to operate on your detached retina to save money? I don't think so.

I would also avoid using somebody that knows you and your soon to be ex-spouse personally. *Your* lawyer should be working for *you* and looking out for *your* best interests.

I can't stress how important it is to get yourself a competent, fair and trustworthy attorney for this life changing event. This is a very emotional time for you and you may not be thinking very clearly. The decisions you make regarding your divorce will stay with you and your kids for many years after the dust settles. I will say it again, *the decisions you make regarding your divorce will stay with you and your kids for many years after the dust settles.* I can't emphasize this point enough.

Most lawyers will offer a no-cost consultation to go over your case. You are interviewing him or her to represent you. This is when you should be talking specifics regarding how much this will cost you. Find out how big of a retainer they require, how much they charge an hour and anything else you think is important to you. Legal bills can rack up quick, so it would be a good idea to ask if they require the balance be paid every month. This is not the time to go bargain hunting. A good lawyer in this instance is priceless; but, of course, most people do have a budget.

Come in prepared when you meet your lawyer. I had a legal pad with lots of questions written down. I had the same legal pad filled up by the time my divorce was concluded. Questions would pop up in my head all the time, so I pretty much would keep it with me most of the time. I would bring this legal pad with me every time I would have a meeting with my lawyer.

Your lawyer is one of the single most important people you will be dealing with during your divorce. They give you emotional support and hopefully good advice (There is a reason they are called counselors, a good lawyer gives you good advice). They are going to be the center of your universe for as long as it takes to get through this tough time. You have to remember, however, that you are not the center of their universe. Things will pop up that are a big "deal" to you, you're going to have to remember that it is just one more issue from one of his or hers many clients.

Going to my lawyer's office reminded me a lot of going to see my doctor. You get there early and wait. You finally get to see your lawyer and you're armed with all kinds of good questions and pertinent information. Then you realize he or she doesn't have unlimited time with you. They are probably thinking about the clients they have already seen that day and perhaps the trial they just got done with while they're talking to you. There is most likely another sad sack just like you waiting in their outer office.

I remember more than one phone call to my Lawyer for some crucial issues I would need clarification. This is when I became very close to my lawyer's paralegal. They do triage for your lawyer. They will let you know whatever issue you have can wait or needs immediate attention. If you are lucky enough to have a good one like my lawyer did, they will save you plenty of heartache and aggravation.

Try to limit your phone calls to your lawyer. You don't want to be known as the "boy who cried wolf" at your lawyers office. Don't be a pest, but if something important does come up make sure to bring it to your lawyer's attention. Also, most attorneys charge for those calls. You will get an itemized bill from your lawyer on a regular basis. Everything will be charged to you including time on phone calls, time for your lawyer to prepare for meetings and court, court appearances, any written correspondences right down to the stamp and most importantly, face to face meetings with you.

I was very lucky to of found an attorney that wasn't out to make a quick buck. He was genuinely interested in helping my kids and me. He did want what was best for all of us. He was very fair with his billing and often undercharged me for the time we spent together. I would intentionally try to schedule our meetings for the last one of the day. That way I knew there wasn't anybody waiting for our meeting to get done. I should thank my lawyer's wife someday for keeping him late at the office every time we had a meeting.

Legal bills rack up very quickly. Take a good look at your statements from your lawyer. Look for ways to save money. Perhaps you didn't need to call him or her over 50 times in one month. Also, be very prepared for your meetings with them. Try to stay on topic. I did a lot of my leg work. I got my police reports, pictures, financial disclosers, tax returns and anything else that was pertinent to my case for my lawyer. This saved me money.

Your lawyer will be one of your best friends during this event in your life. Keep in mind, sometimes you won't be happy with everything they are doing or telling you and that's ok. You may not get everything or even some of the things you want. You don't need anybody to kiss your ass for $350.00 an hour, unless you're into that sort of thing. They are acting in, or should be acting in your best interests and getting you and your kids out of this storm in one piece.

They are the ones who will remind you of what's realistic when it comes to what you want out of your divorce. Remember the word *realistic*. You have to be realistic about your expectations regarding your divorce. If there are no extenuating circumstances, don't expect to get 100 % placement and custody of your kids. If you make more money, especially a lot more money than your spouse, this is going to cost you in some form of compensation. A good lawyer can help you through this also. If you have any assets, such as money saved through an I.R.A. or other investments, you may be able to use these funds to come to an agreement with your soon to be ex. Again, your lawyer can help you out with these issues.

One of the most important things I can tell you from my experience with my lawyer is, you have to be honest with him or her. You have to tell them everything if they're going to do a good job of representing you. A good lawyer doesn't judge you. The judge will do that in court. You don't want them to be surprised by anything from opposing counsel. So if you have any skeletons, dust them off and get them out of your closet.

CHAPTER SIX

Time to Move Out

I was still working nights and Sam and I were living in the same house. About a month had gone by since that fateful morning when Sam announced to me she no longer wanted to be married to me. She was having difficulties finding a place to live in the picturesque suburb she wanted to call home. You would have thought she would have worked out that little nugget before starting this mess. Remember me talking about having an "exit strategy?" Sam had none. If you want to leave somebody, it's a good idea to have a place to leave for. The tension was mounting, as you could imagine. We had a hard time being in the same room together, and I would find any excuse to stay away from the house when I wasn't working.

I started to date when Sam told me she no longer wanted to be my wife. I won't go into the details, but it probably wasn't the smartest thing I have ever done. That on top of a bunch of other issues that made it unbearable to live with her anymore. I didn't want the kids to witness Mom and Dad yelling and screaming at each other on a regular basis. So with a duffle bag in hand, I moved in with two good friends of mine. Ronan and Sharon let me bunk in their basement.

If one of you has filed for divorce, it's a good idea for one of you to move out. I took the high road, and I'm glad that I did. This is a very volatile time; you're better off keeping your distance.

Ronan was a fellow police officer that I had known for years, and his wonderful wife Sharon did their best to make this bad situation bearable. Sharon was from Ireland, and we had a lot in common. We were best of friends. They had a young daughter, Mary. She was a perfect little girl. I was lucky enough to be included in their daily routines, and this always made me feel good.

I was literally the "Creature That Lived under the Stairs." I wound up in the guest room in the basement sleeping on a couch. I was starting to have severe financial difficulties, and it was difficult just to keep my phone on. Here I was a with a good paying job and could pretty much buy anything I wanted about a year ago, to broke and no permanent home. I felt like I was the king of looserville!

Be prepared for something like this to happen to you when you start your divorce. I thought to myself, "I can handle anything because I knew it wasn't going to be forever." You have to keep in mind that there will be temporary situations like the ones I just discussed. Just like a giant kidney stone, this too shall pass!

It took about four months for Sam to eventually move out of my house. (More on that later) I would go over there when I knew she wasn't going to be there or spend time with the kids. Not seeing my kids on a regular basis was the most difficult thing for me during this process. It blew a hole in my heart that has never healed.

I retained my lawyer (Brian), and he advised me that we would be having a preliminary hearing in a couple of weeks. This would take place before a court commissioner. This would be the first time I would meet Sam's lawyer and see her in a court setting. The purpose of this hearing is to set up "temporary" child support, custody and placement of children. If you can agree to everything before the hearing, you don't have to have a pseudo-trial. Your lawyers just present their agreement to one of the many commissioners, and it gets rubber-stamped.

It used to be that if you had two kids that would equal 25% of your check taken out for child support awarded to the parent who had primary placement of the children. It's not the letter of the law anymore, and it differs by state. I was still working nights so I couldn't get 50/50 placement. Even if they spent equal time with us, I made more money so I would have to give Sam some of my paychecks. This is one of the things to discuss with your attorney before a hearing like this. If your very lucky, you can work out an agreement with your soon to be ex-spouse. Anytime you can work out any kind of agreement without a long drawn out battle between your lawyers; it's a win.

If you start coming to agreements, no matter how small of an issue, you will obviously save money and more importantly, you will start mediating issues without outside help. It doesn't hurt though to get the opinion of your lawyer on big issues you have mediated.

Try to keep the lines of communication open with your soon to be ex-spouse with civility and respect. Again, don't be an asshole or a bitch. Sam's lawyer told her not to talk to me about any issues regarding the divorce. That was just one piece of moronic advice he gave her, along with many other ill-fated tidbits of advice.

I realize that there are instances where it will be impossible to accomplish open lines of communication and mediation with your soon to be ex. You will need a very good lawyer in these instances. He or she will be worth their weight in gold.

CHAPTER SEVEN

Your First Court Appearance

Time went by, and I found myself at the top floor of the courthouse where all the family courtrooms were. I met Brian and he reassured me this preliminary hearing would go smooth.

Sam came in, and we said some awkward hellos and waited for her lawyer to show up. He was late and looked frumpy; he literally looked like he slept in his suit. We all shook hands and Sam and her lawyer, "Mr. Frumpy" went out into the hallway for a conference. Brian and I sat together, and he told me that we needed to come to an agreement because the court commissioner that would hear our case if it came down to that, almost always sided with the female.

Sam and Mr. Frumpy came back, and Sam sat down at a table across from me. The two lawyers went out in the hallway to try to work things out. We sat at different tables, and she looked nervous and guilty. I understood the nervous part; I was also, but why did she look guilty?

Brian and Mr. Frumpy came back from the hallway and Brian motioned me to meet him in the hallway. Brian's face was red, and I could tell he was upset. Brian looked at me and asked me, "Is your wife crazy?" He went on to explain that Mr. Frumpy was asking for supervised visitations when I had the kids. "What the fuck!" I yelled out loud. I thought to me, "That's for assholes that are child abusers or drug addicts." There had to be some kind of eminent danger in the house to the children. None of this applied to Sam or me. I looked at Brian and asked him what he said to Mr. Frumpy when he said that. "I told him to go fuck himself!" If there was ever any doubt if Brian was the right guy for the job, this erased that immediately. Brian went on to explain that Mr. Frumpy backed down immediately and they worked out everything else.

Why would Mr. Frumpy throw out such a wild accusation? I have never abused my kids. This was absolutely ludicrous. Sam had never accused me of this kind of behavior, why did this come up now? I have spanked my kids and I'm not afraid to discipline my children. It was always age appropriate and within reason. I believe that's part of being a good Dad. I have never condoned child abuse. I have to deal with abusive parents at work and every time I do it makes me sick.

The amount of child support I would start paying once Sam moved out of the house was a little more than 25% of my salary. He reminded me again that the court commissioner that would hear our case may give her more. He advised me to settle with the amount Mr. Frumpy threw out. I thought to myself, "This won't last more than six months, I can do anything for six months." I was also working on getting on the day shift, so I could share placement and custody of the kids. I knew when that happened I have to pay Sam some amount of money, but it would be substantially less.

I couldn't have been more wrong about everything! The divorce took about two very long years to complete. That was a long time to be semi-separated from my kids. I will never get that time back. I should have thought and planned for the very worse and be pleasantly surprised when things went smooth.

I agreed with Brian and we went back to tell Sam and Mr. Frumpy we had a deal. Mr. Frumpy couldn't wait to run down to the clerk's office to file the paperwork so Sam would start receiving money from me. He had a very smug smile on his face showing his coffee stained teeth when he looked at me. Sam couldn't look at me. She had a look of total shame on her face, which she deserved.

Sam and I met a while later back at my house. Either of us did not plan this. We had to change clothes, and she had to get back to work. I told her I have known some real losers that do a bad job of impersonating a lawyer, and hers was a complete joke. I told her that he was out to make a quick buck and wasn't professional or ethical. This will only make things worse for all of us. Of course, Sam told me I didn't know what I was talking about and left the house in a big huff.

Sam finally found a place in the suburbs that suited her. Actually her folks found a place for her. They bought her a house. It was less than ten minutes from my house, so that made things very convenient. I found it very advantageous to live close to the kids, and it made the transition from living at the home they lived in all their lives to splitting time with a new home that was foreign to them. I realize that's not always possible, but I feel it works better for the kids. Remember kids will forget homework, medicine, favorite toys or stuffed animals. Try to make sure they have all their "stuff" when you pick them up, but there will be times when you might have to make a trip in the middle of the night for a favorite stuffed animals or toy. Being close makes it easier for everybody.

A couple of days after the initial hearing where Mr. Frumpy showed his true colors Sam woke me up before she went to work. She looked at me and started speaking in a subdued tone, as if she was about to start crying, "It must have been horrible for you to have heard what my lawyer suggested." She went on to explain that she never told him that I wanted you to have supervised visitations with the kids. It was his idea to try this tactic.

I actually believed her and started to feel better about things. I was so wrong! It was all lies! She and this lawyer would pull all kinds of crazy stunts in the months to come. This craziness continued for almost a year until Sam fired Mr. Frumpy. I knew after meeting him for a couple of minutes that this guy was a complete joke of a lawyer. That was a year of heartache and pain for my kids and me; not to mention a lot of money wasted.

I can't stress enough how important it is for you to have an honest, competent and professional lawyer working for you. If your lawyer wants you to lie and manipulate children like Mr. Frumpy did, it's time to get a new lawyer.

The day before Sam was moving out of my house we talked about her moving out of my house. I told her to be fair when she took things out of my house. I realized that she would have the kids more at first, so I thought she would take a few more necessities. ***This would turn out to be one of the biggest mistakes of my divorce! Sit down and figure out everything you want to split up with your ex.*** If you don't come to some agreement, make it a part of your final settlement. Once those items are out of your house, it is most likely you will never see them again.

I went to visit my friend Frankie over the weekend when Sam and her helpers cleaned out my house. I do mean they completely cleaned out my house of anything of value. I came home Sunday night to a complete disaster area. The only thing she kept was the dogs and piles of garbage all over my house. The only possessions I had left were a torn up couch, chair and a 15-year-oldTV that worked some of the time. I had some dishes and my clothes that were left in garbage bags and a dresser that was too big for them to get out of the house.

I walked around the house a couple of times with my dogs following me in total disbelief. "How could Sam be so selfish?" I thought to myself. I actually cried for the first time that I could remember. The only person I had to blame was myself. I shouldn't have trusted Sam to do the right thing. The only good part of that night was she was gone for good.

No more tears for me. "This will be the last time I will be taken advantage of by Sam during this divorce." I thought to myself as I paced around my empty house for hours. Eventually, things will get replaced. But I had to live. It was horrible not even having any appliances or a bed to lie in.

I later discovered that the house that her parents bought for her came with appliances. That hurt a lot. I would have the kids also, and they would have no place to sleep and would be totally embarrassed to have any friends over. Then it occurred to me that was Sam's intent all along. Being a vindictive bitch won't get you anywhere in a divorce. It just makes you look like the vindictive bitch you are.

There are no big secrets during a divorce. It is a very transparent process. Especially when the court ordered entities enter the picture. If you're an asshole or a bitch, everybody will find out and will treat you like what you are.

CHAPTER EIGHT

Mediation and More Court Appearances

As time went on I was happy to be in my house, even if it really didn't have anything in it. I did, however, start to feel sorry for myself and grew very depressed. I suggest that you take advantage of any kind of support, both emotionally and financially during this period. If your employer has some kind of employee assistance program or peer support network take advantage of it during this rough patch. Or just ask your general physician, they might have some referrals that take your insurance or suggest a therapist that works at a discounted rate or free.

I wound up asking my parents for money. This was not one of my proudest moments, but it was very necessary. The kids weren't spending the night at my house, and I didn't blame them. I couldn't have them sleep on one couch or a chair. I only saw them when I took them out to eat and go to their sporting events. This is not enough. I felt very distant from them, and this was a time when they really needed me. I had to swallow my pride and think of them.

I got some money from my folks, and I started to refurnish my house and eventually the kids were spending the night with me. Thank you, Mom and Dad! You have to remember that divorce is very tough on your kids. They will need a lot of attention and support from the both of you. I didn't realize it, but Sam and especially her crazy

Mom were trash talking me on a regular basis during this time. This did and will always kick you in your ass. As it did for Sam

It is very important that you do not resort to speaking poorly about your soon to be ex or their parents in front of your kids. Even if they are the biggest idiots in the world; to your kids they are still Mom, Dad, Grandma or Grandpa. All that does is hurt their feelings. They have enough going on seeing their Mom and Dad split up. Any kind of beef you have with any of them should be kept between all of you. Keep your kids out of it!

If your kids bring up the fact that your spouse is speaking poorly of you in front of them, tell them you're sorry they have to hear this stuff. Tell them to tell your soon to be ex to stop please while they are in the room. If they continue this practice, suggest to your kids they leave the area when they start that kind of talk. Hopefully, your trash talking spouse will get the hint. I would also suggest that if this is becoming a regular thing, speak to your spouse and tell them to stop. Explain that it is hurting your kids' feelings and they look like complete idiots when they engage in this negative behavior. Another excellent resource for these situations is your lawyer. Unfortunately, they have heard of this kind of behavior before and should have some helpful ideas for you.

A few months passed and we found ourselves in court for our initial appearance with the judge. This was an official hearing complete with a very kind judge that looked like somebody's cool Grandpa. I was very used to courtrooms, but I'm sure it was a daunting experience for Sam who was never in a courtroom before. This was a hearing to see how the divorce was progressing. Of course, ours was not! The judge ordered mediation at both of our expense.

After the 15 minute hearing, the kindly judge took off his robe and came down to talk to Sam and I without our lawyers. He told us that it would be better off for everybody if we came to an agreement sooner, rather that later. I shook my head knowing that Sam would never agree to anything without a fight, and she smiled at the judge and nodded her head in agreement.

If you can't figure out how to split your belongings and how to share custody and placement of your kids the judge will order mediation. Mediators are usually lawyers that practice family law. I heard all kinds of stories from friends about them. Most of the folks that wound up going to one had positive experiences. The biggest thing to remember when you are going to mediation is; you have to be willing and open to *compromise*. That means there will be a give and take on both sides. Not one side doing all the taking and the other side doing all the giving.

Sam and I wound up at the mediator's office on a weekday night a couple of weeks after the court appearance. He introduced himself and a local law professor that was doing some research on mediation. The good professor requested to sit in on our session. She was there strictly as an observer and would not interfere. Sam and I agreed to her being there, and we began.

The focal point of our mediation was the kids. I discovered that Sam wanted primary custody and placement of our kids. I, of course, wanted to split the time evenly between Sam and me. I believed and still believe that kids need both of their parents unless there are abuse issues.

Sam had some very implausible excuses for her to have the kids almost full-time. I came prepared for these and shot her down with logic. Try to speculate what objections your spouse is going to bring up before you go to the mediation. **Be prepared!** Go over these scenarios in your head before you step foot in the mediator's office. Figure out what's really important. To me, it was my kids.

Again, don't be an asshole or a bitch. I didn't raise my voice when I shot down Sam's very weak excuses that she had prepared. Some of her reasons to get awarded full custody and placement were; one of our son's had a slight learning disability, and she said he would be better off if he didn't share placement with the two of us. I contacted the doctor who was an expert in this learning disability about a week before our mediation, and told him of our impending divorce. The doctor who was an expert in his field of practice said it would not be good for Sam to have sole custody and placement of our son. I thought Sam may use this as a bargaining chip and of course she did. I told the mediator what the good doctor told me and looked at Sam and told her she really didn't have an argument. She also stated that I was working nights, and we couldn't share custody and placement of the kids. I explained that I was in the process of going to the day shift and would be able to have the kids at night. She even tried to use geography. She told the mediator that I lived so far away from her and the kids' schools; it would make more sense for her to have them full-time. I checked out Google Map and got exact distance measurements from my house to important places that the kids were at on a regular basis; so all of her arguments were shot down with logic.

I could see the frustration in her face building with every wrinkle and scowl. She eventually pulled out a yellow legal pad out of her bag. She was very nervous, and her voice started to crackle. Sam looked at the legal pad and said, "My husband can't have the kids full-time because he is verbally and physically abusive towards me and the kids" I thought I was going to fall off my chair. "This bullshit again?" I thought to myself. Sam wouldn't look at me. This was totally scripted, and I knew this came directly from Mr. Frumpy and Sybil, Sam's Mom.

When she said this, everybody in the room looked directly at me in aghast. I knew my best defense to these outrageous and false accusations was to ask for specific examples. Sam, of course only had two instances where I raised my voice at the kids or disciplined them. I explained to her those two examples were not child abuse. I asked for more examples, and she had none. I guess Mr. Frumpy didn't count on me using logic and I'm sure he wanted me to lose my temper and make a scene. Stick to logic and keep your cool if your soon to be ex starts to throw outlandish claims your way.

I looked at the mediator, who was a lawyer and should know the law, and asked him to please explain what child abuse is to Sam. He said he couldn't get involved and had to stay neutral. I was just asking him to state the fact to Sam. He refused and the mediation was over.

Didn't he see the complete lunacy of Sam's argument? If I was truly a "child abuser" why would she want me to have the kids at *any* time? No Mother in their right mind would think that was ok. He was a horrible mediator, and that was a complete waste of everybody's time.

Sam and I wound up on the same elevator leaving. She couldn't look at me. I started the conversation with, "What the fuck were you thinking?" I went on to explain that this is her big strategy; it was seriously flawed to say the least. When we were getting off the elevator, she looked at me and said, "I'm so sorry, I didn't mean any of that." She darted out of the elevator and ran to her car into the night

I stood in complete disbelief for a few minutes and thought to myself, "Is this some horrible dream?" I couldn't believe she would sink this low. I was certain that I.A.D. would be knocking on my door and would be arresting me soon. I thought for sure the mediator or the professor would have run to the police and reported me. I was wrong. That never happened, but it was just another worry to stack in the proverbial pile of shit that was forming in my life.

I knew other police officers whose wives accused them of child abuse and other things that were not true at all. They knew even accusations, no matter how Un-true, could destroy a career in law enforcement. Now I was in the club.

Things were going to get worse before they got better. You have to keep your cool when dealing with your ex, lawyers and especially the judge or any court appointed representatives. It's hard to do when your spouse of 20 plus years is outright lying, but you have to. A big part of these proceedings is measuring your credibility. If you're yelling and swearing in court or to a court-appointed representative, you will lose credibility and whatever you want to the head, even if it's the truth, will fall on deaf ears. Be prepared for anything! Your soon to be ex-spouse wants to win. He or she will also be influenced by many people trying to "help" her out.

Stick to logic and be calm. If you are going to accuse anybody of anything, you better have some proof, or you're going to look like a fool.

CHAPTER NINE

Guardian Ad Litem

I was back in Brian's office, and I told him all the gory details of our mediation. His face turned red when I told him what she accused me of, "What the fuck is wrong with your wife?" he blurted out.

He went on to explain to me that he would be requesting a Guardian ad Litem for this case. I had no idea what that was. He explained that when a couple that is going through a divorce can't come to an agreement regarding the placement and custody of the children, the court will appoint a Guardian ad Litem. They act as the children's lawyer and will do what they feel is in the best interest of the children.

I certainly didn't like the sounds of that. A complete stranger deciding the fate of my children, nope I didn't like that at all. If we didn't ask for one, one would have been appointed by the next time we had court, which was coming up soon. Brian knew I didn't like the idea of a Guardian ad Litem and said, "Hey, why don't you meet Sam at a Starbucks with a legal pad and hammer? This thing is out between the both of you. Why make us lawyers rich?" He was a very good guy and I called Sam and arranged a meeting at a one of the many Greek diners in our city. If you're going to try to have a meeting like this, you're soon to be ex, make sure it is in a public place with lots of witnesses. This is a very volatile time, and emotions are going to be running high.

This was my last chance to mediate with Sam informally before the courts would be deciding the fate of our children. It was crucial to me to get this taken care of before things got way out of control. Sam is one of the most competitive persons I know. Sam was a product of an overbearing father who told her she was never quite good enough in sports or anything else she tried. Nothing but first place was good enough for him. So she was always trying to "win" no matter the cost. Unfortunately, Sam thought of this divorce as a competition that she had to win, no matter who she hurt or the consequences; even if that meant hurting our kids.

She came into the dinner that night with a smug look on her face and a legal pad in her hands. We both agreed that we didn't want a stranger deciding the fate of our kids. I started to lob some softballs her ways, like when we would have the kids for what holidays and agree we would have our kids on our birthdays and Mother and Father's day.

Things were going ok, and I decided to steer the conversation towards the biggest sticking point of the divorce, the placement and custody of the kids. "I'm willing to offer you eight nights, and I will have six nights with the kids every two weeks." I told her with as much sincerity as I could muster. She looked at the legal pad she brought with and stared me in the eyes and said, "No way!" I went on to explain to her that this was my olive branch to her and it was a "one-time-offer." The next time I will be going for 50% and will get it. I started to feel my blood pressure rise and I said to her, "Do you really think it's ok for me to have the kids two nights out of fourteen?" She just looked at me and kept saying, "I'm not going to change my mind."

There comes a time when reason and logic no longer matter when you're trying to reach an agreement, and there is only one of you who wants to reach an agreement. This had turned into an exercise in futility. Both of our voices were raising, and we were making our waitress' evening a little more interesting. It was time to leave before this all got out of hand.

Our next court appearance came, and we were in the same courtroom with the same judge. We were all at our perspective tables with our lawyers and the judge entered. Mr. Frumpy requested a sidebar with the judge. The judge, Brian, and Mr. Frumpy went into his chambers that were directly behind his chair. They did not close the door all the way, and I was trying to hear what was being said. I sat at my table and Sam sat at hers. We were both stone cold silent and stared ahead trying to make out what was being said in there.

"Enough of this bullshit!" I heard coming from behind the semi-closed door of the chambers. It was Brian's unmistakable voice. I could then hear the nice judge give a stern warning to Mr. Frumpy and they all stepped out of the chambers. That is not the time for you to jump up and ask the judge what the hell is going on. You have to be on your best behavior in the courtroom. Even if it is your first instinct to find out what the hell is going on. Let the lawyers do their jobs.

Court was back in session, and the judge ordered a Guardian ad Litem to the case. We were all dismissed and walked out of the courtroom without looking at each other. Brian and I went on the elevator at the same time, and he told me that Mr. Frumpy attempted to go the "Abusive Father" route with this case; even though that wasn't the case at all. The judge told Mr. Frumpy to stop with the accusations unless he had some proof. Obviously, he had none and told him to knock it off.

This is why it is so important to have a good lawyer representing you. I told Sam that this guy was a joke of an attorney. You do not want to make wild accusations in these cases. "Just the facts." just like Joe Friday would say from Dragnet. When you make a serious accusation like these that are baseless, all you do is make yourself look like a fool and you lose all creditability. If your lawyer insists on this strategy, it's time for a new lawyer.

Lawyers have a certain mystique in our society. They are people just like you and me and like any person doing a job; some are better at it than others. Don't be afraid to tell your lawyer that you don't agree with what they are doing. Stick to honesty and integrity during this time and demand the same of your lawyer.

CHAPTER TEN

Stress, And How to Deal With It

You will be under an extreme amount of stress during your divorce. There is no getting away from that fact. Every divorce is different and some are more stressful than others. It's how you deal with this stress that is very important.

I had the stress of going bankrupt; almost losing my house; my kids being confused and sometimes hating me; almost never seeing them; being very broke; losing almost all my worldly possessions; changing shifts and work locations; deep depression; my parents not approving of my divorce; being accused of horrible things by my wife that were not true; a horrible insomnia, and thinking I.A.D. would be coming to arrest me at any moment for something I never did..

The only solace I could take from this was I knew I was not alone. There were folks out there that were going through the same stuff or had it much worse than me. But more importantly, I knew this was a *temporary* situation. Things would eventually get better. I had to remind myself of this fact quite a bit and if you're going through a divorce remember that also.

When I was at my lowest, I thought of how when you are getting ready to take off in a plane and the flight attendant goes over all the safety features of the plane. If there is a loss of cabin pressure or a big hole appears in the roof the oxygen masks will drop down in front of you. Hopefully, you won't be sucked out of the plane and you can put one of those bad boys on. They say that you should put yours on first, and then help your children with theirs. That goes against all good parenting instincts you have. But you're no good to your kids or anybody else if you're out of the picture either physically or mentally.

I wound up going to my doctor with a bad case of the flu after I was about six months in the divorce process. He knew me well and could tell I was not doing well at all. We talked for about 15 minutes about all the divorce stuff and he suggested that I go on an anti-depressant. I didn't want to, but I thought, "What the hell, why not maybe they will help." I tried them for a while and didn't like them at all. I believe they can be a huge help for lots of people, but it wasn't for me. He also referred me to a Psychologist that I visited one time. The shrink told me that I had a good sense of humor about all of this stuff and sent me on my way. I knew he was there if I wanted to go back for help. My doctor also prescribed sleeping pills for me. I would pace the hallway outside of my bedroom almost nightly, and I was a train wreck. You need sleep, or you will fall apart.

I strongly suggest that you get a physical examination when the divorce process kicks off. Talk to your doctor about your physical and emotional health. Don't be afraid to visit him or her when things start to go wrong with you.

Your family doctor can be a very valuable asset during this time mine certainly was.

This will also be a time to lean on your friends and family. There's nothing wrong with that, and they are expecting it. Be careful, though, don't start telling your deepest darkest secrets and problems with a friend or family member that still feels some allegiance to your soon to be ex. Those tidbits can make their way back to the ex very quickly. I was very lucky to have such great friends during this time. My parents really didn't understand it, and I really didn't want them to worry too much. Besides, my Mom already thought I had a one-way ticket to hell because I was getting divorced; she didn't need extra calluses from saying extra rosaries.

There will be "pity parties" that you will be throwing for yourself. Keep them to a minimum. It's very easy to start feeling sorry for yourself. I suggest having loyal friends around and a designated driver. Most of these occurrences happen when there is alcohol involved. One of the biggest mistakes I have observed over the years from folks going through a divorce is the abuse of alcohol. It's very tempting to climb into a bottle of booze every time you start feeling bad. Unfortunately, this is the time when you start making very poor choices. Getting a D.U.I. or other trouble with the law will not help you out. If you're going through a custody battle, like I was, your behavior will be closely scrutinized. Don't give your soon to be ex any ammunition to use against you!

My biggest stress reliever was going to the gym. I spent most of my adult life being a gym rat and it was my time to get away from it all. This proved to be very helpful during this challenging time in my life. If you don't belong to a gym, you might want to join one. If that's not your cup of tea, there are all kinds of stuff you can do for exercise that is very simple and inexpensive. Go for walks, if you have a dog take them with. It will do both of you good. Dust off the Trek that has been in a bicycle cocoon in the back of your garage and take it for a spin. Take the clothes off the treadmill or stepper that has been in your laundry room and use it.

Another good stress reliever I found was reading. I was never a big reader, but since my spouse took all the working televisions out of the house and I had no money to buy a new one, I became a reader. I would buy cheap books at the grocery store, and I discovered the library. We had a very nice one that was close by. I would read humorous books and books on self-help. This was a good way to occupy my time when I didn't have my kids.

My good friend Ronan was an avid sailor, and he invited me out on the lake many times. I took full advantage of this and truly enjoyed it. I would take my kids one I could and sometimes went with just Ronan. It was free and a great distraction and me.

Healthy distractions: You're going to need some during your divorce. Be creative and take advantage of these opportunities.

Take care of yourself and try to occupy your time constructively. This will make you a better person and better parent.

CHAPTER ELEVEN

How to Conduct Yourself during Your Divorce

Time marched on, and I found myself in the office of our Guardian ad Litem. In Wisconsin, if the court ordered mediation fails, which mine did miserably, then the court assigns one of these once you can't come to an agreement on custody and placement of children involved in a divorce. The Guardian ad Litem (G.A.L.) will do an investigation and make a recommendation to the judge regarding the placement and custody of the children involved in a divorce. The judge usually follows the recommendation of the G.A.L.

G.A.L.'S are practicing lawyers who are mostly family law attorney. They have a good understanding of the court system and usually know the judges and what they want and expect. They are the children's lawyer and should do what's best, in their opinion for the children.

Sandy was our G.A.L. Sam and I were seated in her waiting room for what seemed like an eternity. Sandy escorted us to her conference room, and we all sat down. Sandy explained the process to us and laid down some ground rules. She explained that she would be fair; she would be present at all court appearances and future mediations; there would be no secrets (whatever I said about Sam she would hear and vice versa.); we would be responsible of her bill 50/50; she would be interviewing the children alone and with us, and she would be giving us questionnaires for our family and friends to fill out regarding what kind of parents the both of us were. She then folded her hands together and leaned forward towards us and said, "Don't even think about lying to me. I've been doing this for a long time, and I can spot a liar from a mile away." I could tell this meant a lot to her. I have had to deal with child custody issues at work, and it is a very messy business. Most of the time one or both parents are lying to you in an effort to discredit the other. It made me sick that adults acted like this and I could see in Sandy's eyes that she had lots of experience with less than honest parents, and it pissed her off.

Sam and I walked out into her waiting room and scheduled appointments with her to bring our kids. I made sure not to walk out of the office with her because I didn't want any kind of confrontation with Sam. So I went to the restroom, and waited about five minutes. First off, I was worried about a female being our G.A.L. I've heard all kinds of horror stories about "man-hating" G.A.L.'s and how a guy didn't stand a chance with them. I did, however, get a good vibe from Sandy. She did seem fair and definitely had a no-nonsense approach that I truly found refreshing. When I was coming out of the restroom I did see some boxes in a closet with clients' names on them. I assumed these were old files and of course, I recognized a few names as fellow cops I have worked with or work with. They were some of the craziest assholes on the job. So this is the impression Sandy has had thus far of cops. "This is not my lucky day." I thought to myself as I left Sandy's office.

I walked out of the lot, and there was no sign of Sam. All kinds of thoughts ran through my head: How am I going to be able to afford this legal bill? Why is Sam being so difficult? *She* is now dragging our kids into this mess. I truly wanted to keep them as insulated as possible from all this ugliness.

Honesty is the best policy when dealing with situations like this. I realized that I was now "under the microscope", and my parenting skills and behavior would be under scrutiny. Being a cop, you're always being judged on your behavior on and off duty. I was used to that and didn't mind all that much. I'm a boring guy, I workout, spend time with my kids and occasionally socialize with friends. If you're not "boring" it's time to start being boring. Everything you do now will be judged. This is not the time to go out and get drunk and start bar fights or get a drunk driving ticket. You will also be judged on what kind of company you are keeping, especially around the kids. If you decide to date when you are going through your divorce, I suggest that you keep that part of your life separate from your kids as much as possible. That's going to be a judgment call for you. (More on dating later on in this book) It is not a good idea to introduce the convicted felon who is on parole for armed robbery to the kids. You would think this is common sense, but some folks they just don't get it.

Please remember there is no such thing as privacy when it comes to social media. I would strongly suggest that you take a break from Facebook, Twitter, Instagram or whatever else is out there like these. There is always a "friend" out there that will be happy to feed information to your ex about your posts. Worse yet, your kids depending on their age will most likely see your posts. I have had friends post their wild antics from the night before or share to the world how they really feel about their soon to be ex. My favorite is the posts rambling on about how much your spouse hates your Mom and what they really want to do to them if they didn't get caught. It is truly astonishing to me that people are that stupid! Remember you are under the microscope. If you feel this burning desire to post on social media, there are plenty of stupid cat videos out there for you to share. You don't want to be sitting in the G.A.L.'S office, or worse yet court in front of a judge explaining your post about how you need "friends with shovels" to meet you by your soon to be ex's house.

You don't want to keep track of your soon to be ex either on social media. I have seen pictures of "new" girlfriends or boyfriends after a couple of days after one filed for divorce. That is rubbing salt in that wound. Don't be that guy or gal. Keep it classy folks. If you want to keep tabs on your soon to be ex, ask yourself why would you want to put yourself through that? You have both agreed to no longer be husband and wife. Your soon to be ex may have moved on quickly. That is their business, not yours. Don't torture yourself with images of the "other" man or woman. Do whatever it takes to get that out of your head. It's poison and will sabotage your divorce proceedings.

You should also be very careful during this time when communicating with your soon to be ex. You should assume your conversations are being recorded, and he or she is saving all your text messages. Keep your conversations as civil as possible and if you feel like you're going to say something stupid, take a deep breath and either hang up or continue with civility and courtesy. If you are drunk and or feeling emotional, stay away from your phone and certainly don't have face to face interactions with your soon to be ex. You can bet that you will be explaining your poor behavior and judgment at a later date.

CHAPTER TWELVE

Kids and Meeting with the Guardian Ad Litem

I found myself in a meeting with my lawyer Brian. He was growing tired of this divorce, as was I. He introduced the idea that I have the kids six nights out of fourteen and Sam would have them eight nights. I was not ok with this at all. He also recommended that we still go for the 50 / 50 split for custody. Of course, I was ok with that. I could tell he was growing very frustrated with Sam and her idiot lawyer. I told him I was not happy with the uneven split of placement. Remember to let your lawyer know if you're displeased with their suggestions. Really, it's ok to disagree. Just remember to listen to what they have to say and they have a lot more experience with divorce law.

He switched topics, and we discussed the upcoming meeting I had with my kids at Sandy's office soon and then later that week Sam and I were going to have a mediation with Sandy. My head was spinning with wild ideas of how the kids were going to react to this. It made my stomach ache. I didn't want to hurt them, but I was trying to do what I felt was best for them. I walked out of his office wondering if I was making the best decisions.

Make sure whatever decisions you make, keep the best interest of your kids your priority. Listen to your lawyer and also, listen to your gut.

The time came, and I found myself in Sandy's office with my boys. They were anxious and looked confused. There was candy in the waiting room, so that made things a little better. They were here with Sam a week before, but I didn't ask them anything about their meeting. I felt it was best that way, if they wanted to volunteer information about it I would just listen and keep it at that.

We were around a conference table with Sandy and my kids were eyeing the candy that was in the middle. Sandy was very good at putting everybody at ease. They both had big smiles on their faces quickly, and everybody in the room was comfortable. I could tell Sandy had done these types of meetings before and was very good at it. She started out with what our days were like together and how school was going. She also went into extracurricular activities they were involved in. She had a good dialogue with the kids and also asked about what chores they were responsible for. We were cracking jokes and actually were having a good time together.

Sandy then had me leave the room, and she talked to the kids without me. It was a very unsettling feeling sitting out in the waiting room while a stranger was asking about me. They came out of the conference room with Sandy about 15 minutes later. Everybody had smiles on their faces, and the kids had candy in their hands. Sandy took me off to the side and complimented me on my kids. She told me that they were perfect gentlemen and very well mannered.

Sandy walked us to the door, and she reminded me of the meeting I had with Sam and her the next week. I shook my head in agreement, and we all went on with our day. Make sure you don't interrogate your kids about what was said when you weren't in the room or when they had the meeting with your spouse. They're going through enough, and they don't need you grilling them about their conversations when you're not there.

A week went by, and I found myself back in the waiting room of Sandy's office sitting across from Sam. We didn't say a word to each other, and it all felt very clumsy. Sandy came out and walked us back to her conference room with a big smile on her face. Sandy was very upbeat, and I believe she had hoped that her mood would transfer to us.

I was nervous because a lot was riding on this meeting. Sandy was going to tell us what she would be recommending to the judge regarding placement and custody. Sam and I had returned the questionnaires to Sandy before the meeting. I could only imagine what her Mother said about me. I guess she portrayed me somewhere in between Satan and Hitler. I never saw her questionnaires and my family and friends kept their comments very honest and to the point. I have great friends and family, very classy folks indeed.

If you wind up passing out questionnaires like these, tell the people that are getting them to keep it civil, respectful, and most importantly, tell them to be honest in answering the questions. That also goes if you know the G.A.L. will be contacting them. They're not going to help you if they lie and are found out about their Un-truths later. Anything extreme will make you look pretty foolish. You can convey the fact that Grandma is completely bat-shit crazy without using those words. You can also convey the fact that the kid's family members had inappropriate outbursts or other bad behavior. Just have them stick to the facts. The only exception would be if they knew first hand of abuse or neglect. Then they should have been calling the cops. If they did call the police, they could say that.

Sandy started the meeting by telling us that the boys were very well mannered and good kids. She also told us that they had nothing but good things to say about both of us. Sandy also told us that according to the questionnaires, both of us were good parents. Sam was grimacing while Sandy was saying all of this. I'm sure nothing would have made her happier if she told you I was this horrible parent and human being. Sam had to "win."

Sandy leaned over a little bit and stood up straight in her chair and said, "I'm going to recommend that Sam have the kids eight nights and Liam has them six nights out of fourteen. Custody will be 50/50." "Shit! That's where Brian came up with those numbers." I thought to myself. Sam's face was red, and she blurted out, "No way!"

The smile disappeared from Sandy's face and she asked why. Sam went on a typical rant about how I'm abusive and an all-around horrible person. Sandy asked for specifics regarding the abuse, and Sam told her the same stories that she told the mediator that we went to before. Except this time this lawyer actually explained the law to Sam. Sandy looked her in the eye and very calmly explained what she was describing wasn't abuse at all. She looked at Sam and told her a parent has the right to discipline their children. Sam continued her rant and raves and pissed off Sandy.

This meeting was over, and there was no hope of salvaging it. It started out as a meeting and wound up a mediation that didn't work. Sandy stood up and motioned us to the door. You really don't want to call the G.A.L a liar and tell her she didn't know anything about the law. This is the person that is deciding your kids fate and in turn, yours. Sam was rude and completely unreasonable. If you're going to completely disagree with the G.A. L., you should have some real reasons. "No" and "because" are not reasons. These are emotional outbursts that children like to use, not adults. Judges and other officers of the court are not amused by behavior like this.

As we walked out the door together, I stopped Sam and said, "These are not the conditions I wanted, but in the spirit of compromise I will agree to what Sandy is recommending." I looked Sam in the eye and told her this was a gift and a one-time offer. If she walked out on this, I wouldn't agree to it again. Sandy put on a half-smile and looked at Sam nodding at her. Sam looked at Sandy and went on a rant on how she thought Sandy and I were in cahoots, and she was out to get her. It was an all-out temper tantrum. I stood back and let it all happen. Sandy needed to see this part of Sam. She felt as if she was not winning, so she resorted to acting like a spoiled little girl.

This was the second attempt at mediation with a person whose opinion is very valuable to the judge who will make the final determination. If you don't agree with the G.A.L., disagree with respect. Have some pertinent facts to back up your opinion. Even though you're not in a court of law, they are a court-appointed entity, and you should conduct yourself accordingly.

CHAPTER THIRTEEN
"Nesting" and Reconsidering a Divorce

About a week passed, and I found myself waiting outside the same courtroom that I have been in too many times. I always liked to get there early to clear my head and think about what is about to happen and what questions the judge may ask me. I also like to chat with Brian to go over any last-minute developments in the case. I came to enjoy seeing Mr. Frumpy giving me the stink eye while he was going over strategy with Sam. Remember, it's a very good idea to get to court early; I usually was there by about 30 minutes before our scheduled time. The last thing you want to do is show up late for court. You will not make friends with the judge and probably piss off your lawyer.

Brian showed up, and he had nothing new to go over with me. Sandy was next off the elevator, and she was smiling and greeted the both of us. Sam was next off the elevator, and there was no Mr. Frumpy. It turned out that after almost a year of complete bullshit, she fired him. Instead, she had two females with her. Natalya was her new lawyer, and she had an associate with her. Now Sam had a "legal team." Natalya spoke with an eastern block accent, and her associate didn't say anything. Sam introduced them to all of us like she was showing off a new sports car. Sam gave me a smug look of, "You are totally screwed now! Give up now! I have the dream team." Natalya was much more professional looking than Mr. Frumpy and I could tell by the expensive clothes, jewelry, perfectly manicured nails and perfect hair she was all about the money. Just because your lawyer has lots of flashes, that doesn't mean that they are a good lawyer. It was a step in the right direction, and I welcomed anything that would push Sam into reality. (I researched Natalya later and found out her area of expertise was immigration law and she was working at a fancy law firm downtown. She also charged about $100.00 an hour more than most other lawyers in the area. I didn't understand this at all. Why not hire somebody whose expertise is family law when you're going through a divorce? I'm sure she told Sam and her Mom what they wanted to hear. Eventually, Natalya grew tired of Sam and her mother's antics and was ready to quit the case. She did, however, hang in there and make a *lot* of money off of this case)

We all wound up in the courtroom and took our seats at our respective tables. There was a banner on the wall behind the judge that read, "Kids come first!" I know that wasn't there the last time I was here. There was also a different bailiff. Usually, judges keep the same bailiff; maybe his was on vacation or had a sick day.

All rise! Barked the bailiff and out came a shorter black man with short salt and pepper hair with reading glasses perched on the edge of his nose. He sat down, and I thought to myself, "What happened to Grandpa?" I knew that judges in Wisconsin get rotated through different courts, but I didn't see this coming. We had no warning, and this was a little bit of a shock. Judges can be very quirky, and you have to remember it is their court.

This judge was very matter of fact, and I could tell he wouldn't put up with any of Sam's bullshit. He asked where we were with this case and Brian informed him that we tried multiple mediations, and this case was at an impasse. As soon as Brian said that the judge looked at me and said, "What's the problem here?" I was caught off guard a bit but regained my composure. (Remember I said you should be ready for questions coming from the judge?) I explained to the judge that Sam was not willing to negotiate, and she wouldn't even let me in her house when I pick the kids up. I also told the judge that she and her mother would sit far away from me at sporting events and sometimes cause scenes. I told the judge that I thought all of this was damaging to the kids. He took turns scowling at the both of us and said to me, "The both of you aren't co-parenting." I was shocked. I was the one coming with the olive branches and trying to make this as palatable as possible. Sam still came into *my* house, and I really didn't care. I thought it was good for the kids to see Mom and Dad can be civil towards one another. I strongly suggest that you convey the feeling to your kids that Mom and Dad aren't mortal enemies; they are just going through a legal situation.

The judge went on a rant on how he was sick and tired of seeing kids going between houses that the parents lived in. He looked at the both of us and said, "I hear American

Tourister is having a sale on luggage. You might want to get some. If you don't come to an agreement, I will order that the kids stay in one house, and the both of you take turns living in *that* house. Why should the kids have to go back and forth?" This is called **nesting**. That was the first time I ever heard of that, but it seems like a growing trend. I think it would be a total nightmare. I could imagine all the accusations of missing items, things getting broken not to mention down the road if you got re-married. It was a can of worms I didn't want to open. My body went numb with the thought of this.

At that moment, Sandy raised her hand and said, "Your honor, I would like to share my recommendation with the court." The judge barely let her finish her sentence and told her he wasn't interested right now. "This guy is a real charmer," I thought to myself.

The judge shuffled some papers around in front of him and looked up at Sam and said, "There are no allegations of domestic violence or abuse in this case. Why *can't* you split custody and placement 50/50?" I held my breath and fully expected Sam to go on a rant about how I was this abusive bad guy. I was dead wrong. Instead, she blurted out, "My oldest son said he would kill himself if he had to live with Liam!" Natalya grabbed her arm and started to whisper in Sam's ear. I could tell this new bit of information was never shared with her.

My blood started to boil. Since she didn't get her way with the abuse strategy, now she was dragging my kid into this mess. This was the last straw, and I started to become uncorked. I started to stand up and say something; I don't even know what I was going to say and Brian grabbed my shoulder and pushed me back down. He whispered in my ear, "This is not the time." Thank you again, Brian. Another good attribute of an awesome lawyer is to keep you from making a complete fool of yourself, which is what Brian just did.

If he was truly suicidal, I believe she would have clued us in on this information long before today. Judges don't like these types of courtroom shenanigans. I could tell he was pissed. He rolled his eyes at Sam and told Sandy to have my oldest son evaluated by a psychiatrist. He then went on and told us the next time we were in court he wanted to meet the boys. This made me sick to my stomach. Now a guy I don't know will be "evaluating" my kids? This is turning into a complete nightmare.

When we all went out of the courtroom, Brian didn't waste a second and seized the moment. "Do you really want to roll the dice with this guy? Who knows what he will decide if we don't have an agreement." He said to Natalya. She nodded her head in agreement, and they scheduled mediation before our next court date.

Brian being the excellent lawyer that he is, saw an opening and went for it. Natalya took Sam by the arm and whisked her away and scolded her for the "crazy kid" thing she pulled. If you're going to enlighten everybody with a big revelation, such as your kid being suicidal, don't just spring it on your lawyer the first time while court is in session. If you have a specific strategy you want to try out, even though it's complete lies and bullshit, you should consult with your lawyer that is representing you before you step foot in the courtroom; not your Mommy over a cup of coffee.

A lot of court proceedings are a game of who is most credible. I hate to use the word "game", but at times, it does come down to this. I have seen it many times in criminal trials, and it's no different in civil law. You are before a judge, and he or she is actually going to judge you.

I called Sam on my way home and yelled at her for putting the kids in this position. She apologized as she had almost every time she lied during these proceedings. (When we try to get a confession from a criminal in an interrogation, sometimes we let them "apologize" to the victim or the family of the person they just killed or raped. It actually works very well. They might swear up and down they didn't do whatever criminal act they are being accused of, but they might say they are sorry. I know it sounds weird, but it works. Sam fell into this pattern of apologizing for her lies, but would never admit to not telling the truth)

Be ready for the person whom you trusted and loved for many years to resort to all kinds of acts of treachery and deceit to get their way. I know it's like chewing on broken glass, but you have to accept it and cope with this reality. I sincerely hope this will not be the case for you. Sam also introduced the idea of not going through the divorce and staying married. That is not entirely Un-common. ***Remember this, filing for divorce is as serious as it gets. It should never be done in haste and always, after all other avenues of trying to save your marriage are exhausted.*** This is especially important if you have kids together. The only exception I can think of is if there is abuse. You need to protect yourself and your kids.

That was not an option for me. I couldn't live with, let alone be married to somebody that did the things to me and the kids that she did. Perhaps some folks could work things out, not me. You know when something is so broken, it can't be fixed, and that was our marriage.

CHAPTER FOURTEEN

Smear Campaign, How Lies and Deceit will backfire on you.

Wisconsin is a "No fault" divorce state. That means you don't have to prove who is at fault for the destruction of marriage. That does not however, stop folks from attempting to drag their soon to be ex through the proverbial dirt. This also means that almost everybody will be judging your behavior during the time you're going through your divorce and will be digging up old skeletons from out of your closet. I sincerely hope you have a clean break and go your separate ways amicably. Just be ready if that does not happen that way.

You have to remember that during a divorce, especially a messy one, numerous people will closely scrutinize all of your behavior. These include, and are not limited to; the judge, your lawyer, G.A.L., your soon to be ex and their lawyer (who will take unbounded joy in your fuck-ups), family, friends (they might start asking themselves, "Did he/she really do that shit they are accusing him/her of?"), and most importantly and painful, your kids. My soon to be ex didn't hesitate to fill their naïve-little heads with bullshit. I'm glad they saw the ridiculousness of her wild accusations later. But they and I had to endure some bad times when they actually thought I was this horrible person.

Sam had kicked off a smear campaign against me and held nothing back. I didn't know if this was her new lawyer's "strategy", or if she and her Mom thought all this up by themselves. I hoped it wasn't her high price lawyer. I expected more from her.

It started one day when I was at work and received a phone call from Sandy. "Liam, are you calling Sam 50 or more times a day harassing her?" she said (in an I really don't believe this, but have to ask tone), "Hell No!" I blurted out without missing a beat. I had no reason to call her unless it had something to do with the kids. Sandy went on to explain how Sam met with her and told her I was harassing her by calling 50 or more times a day. After I had calmed down, I thought to myself, "This is an easy one; all I have to do is give Sandy my phone records." I have to deal with this kind of stuff on a pretty regular basis in my job, and phone records don't lie. I told Sandy I would have my itemized phone bills on her desk by the end of the day.

I took the records to her office later and highlighted the calls I made to Sam and vice versa. Of course, I never called her 50 times a day, and there were many days I didn't call her at all. There were, however, days that Sam had called me multiple times in one day that made her look like a liar to Sandy. Sandy had inferred that Sam and her Mother had been telling many "tall tales" about me to her. She didn't divulge the particulars, but I could tell she was getting tired of getting lied to. She gave me a reassuring smile and promised me she would have a conversation with Sam about her unfounded accusations.

In the following months a string of occurrences, in which my oldest son would be involved in, would destroy all credibility that Sam had with Sandy.

Unbeknownst to me, Sam had thrown a birthday party for my son's 16th birthday. She invited over 50 kids to her house. What could go wrong with having that many teenagers in one spot? Needless to say the police wound up busting the party and my son and many of the partygoers received underage drinking tickets and some wound up going to jail. Of course, I didn't find this out until later. If your kid gets a ticket or he is involved in something with the police, you're better off telling your soon to be ex. Don't try hiding anything and do not lie about anything like this. You look like an idiot when you don't tell the truth and are found out later.

Sam had also given my son a sports car for his birthday. A very fast sports car! What could go wrong with that? Right? It took about two months, and he and his sports car had a fight with a tree, the tree won. I received the phone call from Sam informing me that our son was in an accident. Something no parent wants to hear. I wound up meeting her and my son in the Emergency room of our local Children's hospital. He was all banged up and needed lots of stitches and glue to put him back together again. She actually hid the car from me for two months. If you have to hide things like that, they're probably not such a great idea. No matter how bad or good of a relationship you have with your ex, you should still be discussing things like what your teenager will be driving, if anything!

Sam still tried to lie to me, even then. She told me that she was borrowing the car from a friend. She also inferred that she didn't know our son was driving it. She came clean a couple of hours later, but didn't show any remorse for her all out lies and didn't take any responsibility for her poor judgment.

I took lots of pictures of my son's injuries and later his ill-fated sports car that was totaled. *Make sure you document everything that you think has some value in proving any inappropriate behavior or choices made by your soon to be ex.*

I eventually discovered the underage drinking party and retrieved the police reports regarding the "big bash." I wound up going to Sandy's office with the pictures and police reports at my lawyers request. She was not happy at all. She had called Sam and asked her about the party and the accident. Sam downplayed the accident and lied about everything else. Of course, while Sam was doing this, Sandy had the police reports and pictures in her hands. I can't stress enough how important it is to be honest during this process, even when you mess up. It's much better to be honest and hone up to your mistakes rather than bold face lying to court-appointed officers. If you're not sure what to do, consult with your lawyer. Hopefully, they will be the voice of reason. Remember you can and will sometimes be an emotional wreck. It is good to have a cool head and voice of reason during these times.

Sandy called me and told me that about Sam's conversation. Sandy also asked me about a tutor my son had been going to when he was younger to help him with his reading. Sam and her mother swore up and down that I never took him and had nothing to do with it. I actually took him every Wednesday during the school year, and Sam took him sometimes in the summer. Silly Sam. Didn't she think I could just ask the tutor? I called the tutor and had a great conversation with her. She remembered me, but didn't remember Sam. I asked her to write a letter or call Sandy and explain how I actually was very involved with his tutoring. She did this for me, and Sam looked like a fool, again.

More lies! This eroded most or all credibility Sam had with Sandy. I started behind the eight ball with Sandy because of my job and all the allegations (that were later proved to be false), and now I was the rock star.

Our next mediation was set on the Friday before Labor Day. One more try to get Sam to agree to the shared placement and custody of the kids. I met Brian in his office, and Sandy was there also. They both had plans for the weekend and were eager to get over this issue. Sandy was not happy with Sam and all of her lies and had a look on her face of she was going to call her out for not telling the truth. We briefly talked about the underage drinking party, the accident and the tutor. Sandy just shook her head and looked pissed off.

Time ticked away, and there was no sign of Sam or Natalya. Brian called Natalya and I called Sam. No answer for either one, just recorded messages. They were no-shows. Sandy had enough and told me she would recommend full placement and custody to me, and Sam would have to pay me child support. We let the dust settle and after some time to let that digest. After more discussion, we all agreed it would be better for the kids if it were 50/50 placement and custody. That's all I ever wanted, and I would be a hypocrite if I changed it.

Stick to your guns and tell the truth during this part of your divorce. Hopefully, it will all work out for you and your kids. It did for me.

CHAPTER FIFTEEN

Helpful Tips for Dealing with Kids during Your Divorce

I wrote this book from the perspective of being a Dad with two teenage boys whom I love very much. I believe you could get something out of this book that will help you even if you don't have kids, but it is geared towards parents going through or have gone through a divorce with kids involved.

There is nothing more important than your kids during and after a divorce. It really is that simple. Everything you do and strive for and settle on during the divorce should be in your kid's best interest. Your job is to be a good parent. You should make that very clear to your lawyer, and they should already be thinking along those lines anyway.

Divorce is a very traumatic event in any kid's life. The most desired outcome is not to get divorced and live happily ever after. Ok, I know all too well that doesn't always happen. There are also marriages that people stay in that aren't healthy for kids also. So if you find yourself in a divorce, make sure to make it as painless as possible for your kids.

I would hope you and your soon to be ex can agree on that. Mine would smile and nod in agreement, but her actions painted a very different picture. She is the most competitive person I have ever known. She had to "win" at any expense, even if that meant her "winning" wasn't what was best for the kids. It was almost impossible to negotiate anything with her in good faith when all she wanted to do was "win."

Looking back on my divorce, I can share the things I did right and wrong during my divorce regarding kids. Here are some tips;

- First and foremost love them unconditionally, even if they don't reciprocate. They are going through a tough time, even if they aren't showing it. Let them know you love them and will be there for them forever. Tell them and show them through your actions. Don't over-do it, though. That will probably freak them out.

- Try not to fight (verbally and of course **never** physically) with your soon to be ex in front of them. This will take some self-restraint. Especially when your other crazy half is starting it and is saying and doing very crazy stuff. Leave the room, hopefully with your kids in tow. Let your soon to be ex be crazy by themselves. That goes for crazy in-laws also. Sam's mother had meltdowns at my kids sporting events on more than one occasion and actually wanted to fight physically with me in front of my kids' basketball team one time. I just walked away and informed my lawyer about her crazy antics. She just looked like a complete loon standing by herself with her old wrinkled fists balled stamping on the ground like a spoiled little child. (I, of course, reported these incidents to my lawyer and the G.A.L. Sam and her Mom denied all of it, even though I got statements from folks in the crowd later about the outbursts and gave them to the G.A.L. More lies from Sam and her Mom.)

- Let your kids be kids. Your kids want to continue their routines through all of this. Mine were teenagers and their friends and activities were a very big part of their world. If your kid usually slept over at a friend's house or spent time with them from time to time, let them continue that ritual. Even if that means you won't see them as much as you would like to. Remember you're not all living together anymore and time is a precious commodity. That means you will probably have to sacrifice *your* free time, hobbies or your work schedule. Sorry, but those all day golf outings every weekend might have to be put on hold for a while.

- *Never* make your kids choose between spending time with Mom or Dad! Kids are very keen to please the both of you. They don't want to make either of you feel bad. Make sure it's in writing when you have your kids. Be very particular and meticulous with this part. Let that be known to your lawyer. This should be very clear when one of you moves out. One example of not having all scenarios in writing was when Sam wanted to have the kids on Father's Day because it was "her" day when we first broke up. Are you fucking kidding me? What you think is common sense and a no-brainer sometimes isn't.

- Keep open lines of communication with your kids. Let them know you're there for them and will help and support them any way you can. It may be a one-way conversation many times, but whatever you're saying they are absorbing.

- Pay very close attention to them during this time and look for obvious signs of trouble; bad grades, being withdrawn, big mood swings are just a few things to keep an eye out for. If you see signs of trouble, share them with your soon to be ex and ask if they see the same things. Sam would never cooperate with me regarding anything like this. She would have seen reporting any of these things as weakness on her part and would never have reported that to me. If you think your kids need help from a therapist or other professional, get it for them.

- If you can, try to give the illusion of Mom and Dad don't hate each other and can be civil towards each other. They obviously know that things are not ok, but try to make it as comfortable as possible for them. If there are sporting events, try to sit by each other. During school activities, you might actually have to sit next to each other, it won't kill you. Your kids are noticing all of these things, even if you don't think they are.

- Do not give your kids any false hope that you will eventually get back together and there will be a big Disney happy ending. Fuck you Disney! I hate those movies. Be realistic and kind to them if they ask about any chance of all of this ending and all of you going back to the way it used to be. They need to cope with the fact that Mom and Dad are not going to live in the same house anymore, and they may eventually get married again to other people. Of course, you will have to consider the age and maturity level of your child when dealing with this. My kids had no false hopes of us reconciling. It was very obvious it was over. I do know some folks that weren't as black and white about all of this and it caused some trouble down the road.

- Remember you still have to be a parent; even if that means you have to be the "bad" guy or girl. It is a difficult time for your kids, and you certainly don't want to hurt their feelings, but sometimes it will happen, and it is for their sake. A good example of this is when my oldest son had numerous concussions in a short period from contact sports. I wanted him to quit because of this long before this, but Sam didn't want him to stop. She lived vicariously through our sons playing of these sports. She had a specific identity when he was playing, and she did not want to give any of this up, even it that meant the health of our child. She also didn't want to tell him "no" and hurt his feelings. Our pediatrician told us he should stop playing these sports, but he stopped short of saying, "He should not play contact sports ever again." I used to like him and wound up resenting him for that. We eventually wound up at a specialist in traumatic brain injuries and he told us under no circumstances should we let him play contact sports ever again. Sam actually leaped towards me in the small exam room because I was taping our conversation with the doctor. She didn't want what the doctor said to us recorded. "Why not?" I thought to myself. The nurse ran out of the room terrified at what happened, and my son broke down crying. It was a hot mess to be sure. Even when this expert gave us his prognosis, Sam still gave my son a false hope that he would play again, making me the absolute asshole. Sometimes you have to be the bad guy in order to be the good parent, always do what is in your children's best interest. Remember that always.

- Do not bad mouth your soon to be ex in front of your kids. It is very tempting to call your wife or husband all kinds of bad names and remind your kids of how much of a train wreck they might be. You have to remember that they are still Mom or Dad. Let your kids have their childhood and their naive outlook on life and their parents for as long as possible. That also goes for grandparents, no matter how crazy they might be. Your kids will form their opinions when they get older, and the truth will come out eventually.

These are just a few pointers I have learned from going through my divorce. One of the biggest changes I have noticed since my divorce is me giving in to my kids or spoiling them more after my divorce. I call it "Divorce Guilt." I feel bad that my kids had to go through this life-changing event and don't want to hurt them any more than they already have. I just have to remind myself that them having extra "stuff" or them getting away with more than they should won't make them better kids or me a better Dad. Don't turn your kids into spoiled brats.

Love your kids and do what is in their best interest. Give your kids the tools to succeed, and never set your kids up for failure. You will make mistakes, but hopefully, you will learn from them be the best Mom or Dad you can be.

CHAPTER SIXTEEN

Sex, Love, and Relationships

If you're reading this book I guess you are thinking about, going through or have gone through a divorce. As I have mentioned earlier in this book, I believe the main goal of marriage is to stay happily married. Sounds pretty simple, doesn't it? Unfortunately, sometimes it just doesn't work out that way.

If you feel your marriage is having problems, do something to fix it! Address the problems directly and don't just hope those things will just "go away" or "get better" with time. The fix could be as simple as bringing up whatever problems you're having with your partner. Try to keep the lines of communication open as much as possible. Little problems can fester and turn into big ones mighty quick. Don't be afraid to suggest going to a marriage counselor. This doesn't necessarily mean your marriage is on life support, but you want to fix what might be wrong. I know most of this isn't very macho. But if you take the macho route, you might be macho all by yourself and paying a big price for it.

Show your spouse with actions, not just tell your spouse how much they mean to you. It's amazing how good you feel when your partner actually listens to you when they are telling you about their day at work or something that is important to *them*. Whatever they are talking about may not be very important to you, but if it's important to your spouse, it should become important to you as well. Show compassion and empathy when appropriate and it will be reciprocated when the time comes. You are the person they should be able to lean on.

Hey guys, try surprising your wife with a meal you prepared ready by the time she gets home from work. Or better yet, take care of the laundry and clean the house before she gets home from work. All of this and a nice foot rub are powerful foreplay tools. You may truly unlock the inner vixen in your mate.

Your wife should be your girlfriend, and your husband should be your boyfriend. I'm a big advocate of date nights. You have to have some time with just your spouse alone. This means getting dressed up a bit and look good for your partner. That means you gals should get out of your sweats and put as much effort into dressing up and hair and makeup for your husband, as you do for the occasional night out with the girls. Guys, yes you should take a shower and shave and put on something other than your favorite jersey or flannel shirt. Just think back to when you were working hard to impress each other when you started dating. You should still be trying to impress and attract your partner. This also means it is time for the two of you to get out of the house for your dates.

Speaking of trying to attract your mate, I don't understand why I see so many women in the gym trying to lose weight and look good when they are newly divorced or going through a divorce. Perhaps this is something you should have been doing all along. The same goes for you guys. I see guys that I have never seen before in the gym and after talking to them, they tell me they are trying to get "back into shape" because they will soon be or are back on the market. Sorry guys, but bowling, golf and softball just aren't exercise. They and other "sports" are excuses to drink beer with the guys and be away from home. I'm a big believer in exercise, and it's obvious benefits to your mental and physical health. The two of you don't have to look like cover models for fashion magazines, but you shouldn't give up and stop trying to look good for your spouse! A gym membership is much cheaper than a divorce.

Get yourself a pool of reliable babysitters you trust and use them. I know it is tough with careers, kids in sports and all their activities, and there could also be special circumstances such as elderly parents or special need children. You have to make the effort for everybody's sake.

A friend of mine told me a story of a young couple he knew that was getting married that has stuck in my head for years and makes sense. They went to their parish priest and had to be interviewed by him before he would marry them. He was an older priest in his 60's with grey hair and a quick wit. He asked the regular questions that you would expect a priest to ask: are you going to have kids? Are they going to be raised Catholic? etc.... After they started to all become comfortable with each other he looked at the young couple and said, "Part of my job is to counsel couples that are having troubles with their marriage. I have learned a lot about relationships, and I have learned there are three things that you must do to keep your marriage together." The young couple both stared at him with big doe eyes and the priest continued, "First, sleep. You have to have enough sleep. If you're sleep deprived, you will be crabby and argue over stuff you probably wouldn't if you were appropriately rested. Second, eat. Too many folks go on these fad diets and are hungry all the time. Again, you will be crabby and irritable if you're hungry. Eat sensibly and avoid being hungry. And third and most important......SEX." They young couple blushed as the priest smiled at the two of them and said, "I have never had a couple come in for counseling if they had an awesome sex life."

The priest may have had a simplistic view of marital bliss, not to mention he probably hasn't been married. But I think the good father is on to something. I do believe a couple can have a rock and roll sex life while they are married. It will, however, take some effort on both your parts and a bedroom door with a good lock on it if you have kids.

Contrary to some negative perceptions from some organized religion, sex is a very good thing. There's been an overabundance of studies on the subject and I believe most of the "experts" say it is good for you physically as well as emotionally.   I can't think of something that connects two married people more than sex.   The act produces all kinds of good chemical reactions and gives you both an incredible feeling of intimacy and closeness that a marriage needs.   If you're having sex with your spouse on a regular basis, how can you stay mad at him/her for not doing the dishes and other silly arguments that may pop up?   I defy you to even think of the dirty dishes after you've had a mind-blowing session between the sheets. Sex is the glue that keeps you together!

I have heard that woman need to feel loved in order to have sex and men need sex to feel loved. I'm sure there are exceptions to that rule, but for the most part, I think it's spot on. So guys and gals do your best to keep those love vibes going and get naked! It's a win-win situation when you and your spouse are making love on a regular basis. (To each other of course)

There is a variety of reasons people get divorced. Many times it's a combination of things; poor communication, unfaithfulness, tragedy, Illness or accident, or you just plain grow apart. When you split up with your spouse, this is a good time to reflect on what you think went wrong. This would be a good time to take an inventory of what you think you may have done to contribute to the ultimate demise of your marriage. Please don't wallow in this. Just try not to make the same mistakes twice. This would be a good time to work on the things you believe you need to improve on and perhaps time to get rid of the things that may have contributed to the riffs in your relationship. A good therapist might be a good idea to help you sort all of this out.

I'm not talking about abuse. If you're in an abusive situation, get the hell out and take your kids with you. Your safety and your children's safety is paramount. This also holds true if your spouse if an addict; drugs or alcohol.

Most folks blame the other person for their marriages going south. Some of the time the blame rests square on one person's shoulders, but most of the time it is a team effort. Remember getting divorced is closing one door and opening another one. Walk through that open door with your chin up with the confidence that you will try not to make the same mistakes twice.

CHAPTER SEVENTEEN

Dating...Ugh!

When my divorce kicked off, I couldn't wait to start dating. After years of a miserable marriage, the thought of being with somebody who actually thought of me as attractive, wanted to have sex with me on a regular basis and actually wanted to be with me was absolutely intoxicating. I jumped into dating with both feet into the deep end of the pool and wound up drowning. The girl I started dating after Sam told me she no longer wanted to be my wife dumped me after about a six-month relationship. It wasn't all bad. As a matter of fact, we had some great times together, it just was not meant to be.

I was devastated and moped around for what seemed like a very long time wallowing in self-pity. I learned a lot about relationships and myself during that time. While this relationship wasn't meant to last, It did show me that another person actually wanted to be with me. If you have been in a long relationship and you were used to your partner pretty much not showing any interest in wanting to be intimate or just close to you, it can be devastating to your feeling of self-worth. I spent many a night tossing and turned thinking to myself, "What the hell is wrong with me?"

You have to give yourself some time to heal and get comfortable with your skin when you're going through or have gone through a divorce. Only you know when the time will be right to jump back into the dating pool again.

It is a daunting task, thinking about going on dates. Depending how long you were married, the idea of dating again after being out of that scene for what could be many years can be absolutely terrifying. How do people meet each other now? Should I try on-line dating? I can't even think about going into bars and asking strangers for their phone numbers. These were just a few notions that were jumping around in my head.

I was in my late 40's and having friends 'fix me up' was pretty much out of the question. Most of my friends my age were married and had kids. They didn't have many single friends to fix me up with. If they were my age never married or had been in a long-term relationship, I couldn't help think to myself, "How many cats does this woman come with?" I have two dogs that would never work. Of course, I'm joking, but I was a guy at the end of a marriage that lasted 21 years and had two kids. I wouldn't have anything in common with a gal that had never experienced any of that.

My divorce was lingering on much longer than what I had originally anticipated. I was feeling very frustrated with the whole process, but was starting to feel pretty good about myself, and I thought it was time to start dating again. I had to go forward.

I gave myself rules for dating. First: No girl would meet my kids for at least six months or until I was officially divorced. Second: I had to put my kids first and any girls I dated second. This meant I would not sacrifice any time with my kids so I could go out on dates. I would only date on the nights that I didn't have my kids. I was shocked by some of the people I knew that would sacrifice time with their kids so they could be with some girl they barely knew. Third: if a girl didn't like rules one or two, they weren't worth my time.

At first, I thought I would just let it happen. I believe girls can pick up a vibe when a guy is self-confident and is interested in dating. I dated a couple of acquaintances, and that turned out "ok." Not much in the way of substance, but, at least, I broke the proverbial ice. It is going to feel weird to be going out on a date after you have spent so much time with somebody else. It will be a little awkward, but that's ok. You need to get the first couple of dates under your belt and don't take it so seriously. This should be a fun time. Try to make it that.

So I got some dating experience and thought it was time for me to try Internet dating. There was no Internet when I was first married, so this was all new to me. There is a cornucopia of dating sights out there. Some are free, and some charge a nominal fee. I decided to try one free and one paid site. I discovered that the same girls were on the free and paid sites after some time.

An important piece of advice to all of you would-be Internet daters is to be safe. Be very careful not to get all emotionally wrapped up with somebody you don't know. Your emotions can certainly cloud your judgment. Start out *slow*. Odds are you haven't been doing a whole lot of dating for some time. There is no big rush! I actually knew people they met on one of these sights and moved in with each other after a couple of months. All of these situations ended in disaster as you can imagine.

Honesty is the best policy. It is very tempting to embellish a wee bit when you are making a profile that a bunch of folks is going to see. It is ok to feel weird about telling a would-be romantic interest how great you are. Just stick to basic facts how old you actually are (the person you go out on a date with will find that out.), be proud of your age. That's lots of experience under your belt. Own it, don't be ashamed of it. Your physical appearance: odds are the person reading your profile doesn't spend every waking minute in the gym either. When you post pictures of yourself, make them recent pictures. Nobody wants to see you in your old "glory" days. We all change, and that's ok. Absolutely no pictures of your kids. Why would you post that? But I actually saw this. It's ok to say you have kids and their ages. Don't give out specifics regarding your children; remember it is very important to be safe. Kids can be deal breakers for some folks. That's ok. It just means they just aren't a good match for you.

When you're navigating the potential minefield of Internet dating, have a sense of humor. It doesn't do anybody any good to take it personally when things don't work out with your date. Chalk these experiences up as learning tools and move on. There will be dry spells and it's ok to give yourself a break from Internet dating if things aren't just working out. It's not going away anytime soon. When I felt down in the dumps about not meeting the right girl I remembered what a good friend of mine said about girls and dating, "Forget about the girl that just didn't work out., Girls are like city buses, if you wait on the corner long enough another one will come along." Remember to keep that sense of humor.

I went out with a variety of girls during my internet dating stint. I actually married a gal I met on an Internet dating site. That story is in my other book. Most were nice girls that just weren't a match for me. Some of them were crazy, and some were criminals. I learned that people are frail creatures and just want to be loved and accepted. I was no different. You have to keep your sense of humor when rolling the proverbial dating dice. Remember to follow your instincts, be safe and always think what's best for your kids.

CHAPTER EIGHTEEN

How to Overcome Stalemates

My divorce had hit a brick wall, and I felt like I was losing my mind. My kids were confused and depressed; I felt as if I was in a state of an almost two-year limbo that was never ending and I was facing horrible financial trouble.

This is when a good lawyer steps in and takes action! That is just what Brian did. Our biggest roadblock was the placement and custody of my children. The G.A.L. recommended 50/50 shared placement and custody, which is what I wanted all along and felt what would be in the best interest of the kids. Everybody was on board, except for Sam. Most of the other particulars of the divorce were already worked out.

We tried last ditch efforts of mediation with all parties that would wind up with Sam crying and pounding her fist on the desk saying, "No Way!" Her attorney trying to convince her she was not going to get her way usually accompanied this. You can only mediate so much. So Brian told me he was going to file a motion for 50/50 placement and custody of the kids. We sat down and drafted the motion and set a court date. A *motion* is a written request or proposal to the court to obtain an asked-for order, ruling, or direction. You're asking the judge to rule on one or more parts of the litigation, not the entire Divorce. This should only be done after failed attempts at mediation. Remember, judges want you to work things out amongst yourselves. If you can't do that, you may be very unhappy with what their decisions can be.

Brian introduced me to his associate, Tony during this meeting. Tony was a lawyer that had recently started to work at this law firm. He was not a partner, but I could tell he did a lot of the grunt work so someday he would become a partner. Tony was a cheery chap that was eager to please. He was tall and lanky with an odor of fresh cigarettes on his person and a sly twinkle in his eyes. I had a good feeling about him. One thing to keep in mind is that a newer lawyer from a law firm usually doesn't charge as much as a partner. Keep an eye on your bill for that. Just because you have retained a lawyer for a case, that doesn't mean you will always get the same lawyer every time there is a court proceeding. This, of course, depends on how big the law firm is that your lawyer is associated with. I was nervous having a new guy introduced into the mix, but I did trust Brian and went along with it.

We had a scheduled a court date for about a week, and this is when the judge would rule on our motion. This is also the day that the judge wanted to meet our children. I found it very unsettling that my kids would be drug into this mess. A courtroom can be a scary thing for an adult, not to mention a kid.

The fateful day came, and we all took our places in the courtroom. It felt a little odd having Tony sitting next to me, but my gut instinct told me he would do a good job. My kids were told to wait outside of the courtroom, and the G.A. L. would bring them in when the judge wanted to talk to them. My blood boiled thinking about how Sam's unwillingness to accept reality forced my kids into this situation. You have to prepare yourself for the fact that your kids might also wind up at a court hearing. I tried to make it as un-scary as possible. I told them the judge wanted to meet them to say hi. They wouldn't be testifying like they see on the T.V. It was just an opportunity to say hi to the judge. Don't surprise your kids with this and be honest.

The judge came into the courtroom and had a seat in his chair, and we all greeted him on our feet like soldiers standing at attention when a general came into a room. He was smiling and said he wanted to see the kids. Sandy went out in the hallway and escorted our kids into the judge's chambers. The judge's voice carried, and I could hear most of the conversation. It was very benign. He asked how school was going and what they wanted for Christmas. This was not the scenario I was expecting. I thought he would be grilling them about which parent they liked best and would ask about how good of parents we were. I had totally misjudged the judge. He was a nice guy and was very friendly with my kids. It didn't take long, and they were escorted out to the hallway by the G.A.L. They both had smiles on their faces, and I felt an overwhelming sense of relief.

The judge put his reading glasses back on and said, "You have two great kids there. They were both perfect gentlemen." He looked at Tony and told him to proceed with his motion. Tony told the judge that he wanted placement and custody modified to 50/50 shared placement. The judge looked at Sandy and asked her if she had any objections to this and she had none. The judge shuffled some papers around and said, "I see no reason why custody and placement shouldn't be shared between Mr. and Mrs. Burke." Sam immediately went into a rant accusing me of abuse. Looking very perturbed, the judge looked at Sam and asked why she didn't bring this up before now. Of course, she didn't have any answer to this because there wasn't any abuse. Sam kept rambling and screaming at the judge. Tony and I just sat there in complete silence and let all of this play out. The judge motioned towards the bailiff and he got up and started reaching for his handcuffs. "Oh my God! Sam is going to get arrested for contempt of court." I thought to myself. Natalya finally got control of Sam, and the matter was concluded.

You have to remember that a court of law is not an open forum to blurt out all of your crazy notions. When a judge tells you to shut up, that is exactly what you should do. A judge's courtroom is his or hers, and they run the show.

The judge slammed his gavel down, and he disappeared into his chambers. Sandy guided all of us into a small conference room, and we signed some paperwork. All of this didn't take more than 15 minutes. All the pain and anguish was over, just like that. I found out later this is what the kids wanted all along. Everybody was happy, except for Sam. This was the last big stumbling block, and our next court date would be our final.

Sam's last bit of ammunition against me was money. She was not ok with the standard child support agreement that the G.A.L. calculated. I had a good pension, and she wanted every bit she could get her hands on and as much money as she could get per month while the kids were minors.

Just because you share placement of the children evenly with your ex, doesn't mean you won't pay child support. If you make more money than the other one, they will get some money every month from you. You have to remember that things are not going to be the same as when you were married and had a decent dual income. You're going to have to be thriftier with your cash. Establish a budget and stick to it.

A couple of weeks later we wound up going to a financial mediator to finish this all off before our next court appearance. I didn't know there was such a thing as a financial mediator. It was very expensive, and Sam got more than she deserved. Of course, the mediation that should have lasted a couple of hours, wound up going all night and she was completely unreasonable. Even Natalya was growing very tired of her antics. We did eventually reach an agreement and shook hands. In typical "Sam" fashion the day after the marathon mediation, she wanted more money. Brian quickly squashed this notion, and our agreement stayed at what we all agreed.

All the difficult parts were done and the kids and myself were adjusting to being together again on a regular basis.

All that was left was the last court date that was looming on the horizon.

CHAPTER NINETEEN

End Game

The time had come to end this nightmare of a divorce. There were plenty of hard feelings and pain for everybody involved. Keep in mind when you are going through the worst parts of a bad divorce, there is ultimately an end. You and all involved will survive and recover from this horrendous event. Even if you have a relatively "easy" divorce, there will still be scars and bad feelings. Take it one day at a time and allow yourself to heal.

Your recovery time will differ depending on your situation. Don't hesitate to get some professional help with this. Remember my airplane story? For you and your kids. Kids are very good at letting you think everything is fine. Keep a very close eye on them in the months after your divorce, just like you have been paying extra close attention to them during your divorce. Look for any warning signs that they are not doing ok. Bad grades, big mood swings, not hanging around their usual friends and self-destructive behavior are just some of the things to look for. It is very hard on them, and they might not let you know how they are doing. When your divorce has ended, there is an inevitable finality to all of this. It may not sink in with your kids right away, but it will eventually. Make sure that you remind them often that you love them and will take care of them.

So we were all back in the same courtroom one more time. This would be our final appearance. I felt a lot of different emotions; anxiety, fear, glee and yes some sadness. I was sad that this took so long and Sam had resorted to some very underhanded tactics to try to get her way. I was sad that a marriage of 20 plus years had gone down the tubes. You don't march down the aisle and say, "I do" thinking it will all end in a firefight later. I was most deeply saddened by how much grief my children had to go through unnecessarily. They were confused and hurt. I never wanted that to happen and tried my best to shield them from all the pain. Sam and her mother did the opposite.

We all wound up at our regular tables and waited for the judge to start the proceedings. The final divorce proceeding is formal; you and your spouse will also have to testify. This was no big deal for me; I have testified in everything from homicides to somebody fighting a speeding ticket. Sam had never testified before, so I'm sure it was very intimidating.

After you are sworn in your lawyer will ask you some very simple questions like; how long you were married, if you're married to anybody else, if you are doing this of your own free will and if the marriage is irreconcilably broken. He also asked if I was satisfied with himself and Sandy during this process. I don't think I was up there for more than ten minutes. Sam followed me, and the questions were the same except she was asked if she was pregnant. Kind of weird, but they will ask you that.

This is **not** the time to be overly dramatic, and you should have everything settled by the time you are at this phase. Sam behaved for the most part, and the judge looked at all of us and advised Sam and myself; we couldn't get married for six months, and the matter was concluded with the pound of a gavel.

We were all ushered into a conference room and signed a small mountain of paperwork. After it was all over the lawyers shook hands with themselves and us. It felt like the end of a football or basketball game my kids were playing when all the teams shook hands and had that "No hard feelings" look about them. Sam just scowled at me, and she and Natalya disappeared into the busy hallway.

I thanked Sandy and Brian for their patience and everything they did for me and the kids. I could tell they genuinely did care about us, and that made me feel good. Brian and I said our final farewells and just like that; it was over.

So now I'm officially divorced and I guess you are or will be soon. Come grab an ore and jump in my canoe. Now, what? You may be asking yourself. It may not hit you right away that you are now a single person. That's fine. You have let yourself take all of this in and give yourself some time.

They say that there are different stages of grief when you are going through and have gone through a divorce. There are different variations, but they are very similar to the stages of grief when dealing with a death of a loved one. Out of the many experts or folks who like to think of themselves as experts, most agree that these stages don't necessarily go in an exact order. When you have moved on to one, you can certainly revert to another. The stages I experienced and you will probably also are as follows:

- Denial: You can't believe this is actually happening. I really didn't have too much of this. It had been coming for some time.

- Pain and Fear This really hurts in many ways and how am I going to go on by myself?...etc emotionally, monetarily. You will feel all kinds of pain during your divorce; some of it will never go away. That's ok, though. Pain lets you know you're still alive; it can be your friend. Pain is also the great motivator. Pain get's you off of your ass and makes you do something to stop feeling sorry for yourself. There was a poster in the academy that read, "Pain is weakness leaving your body!" I thought of that poster many times when I thought I was going to die after running until I felt like I was going to pass out. It's ok to be afraid during this time. My biggest fears were if my kids would be ok during and after all this mess. I also had the fear of losing my home and a host of other financial problems. I made it through all the mess and you will too!

- Anger: How could the person I exchanged vows with in front of God and family and friends be doing this? I don't deserve this. I was angry because Sam made the whole divorce into an epic battle when it didn't have to be. I would add frustration with this emotion. You will experience both. Don't let these emotions make you do something stupid or cloud your judgment too much.

- Bargaining: You might start to promise your spouse things mostly unrealistic, to stop the action. Or you tell yourself you will stop or start a behavior to change this. Please don't embarrass yourself. Odds are the ball is rolling; don't beg your spouse to stop the divorce if it's inevitable. Keep your chin up! You might also start bargaining with God. It's amazing how religious I've seen people get during crises like. "I promise I won't do X if you just let me have my life back." Or the opposite, "I hate you, God! How could you of let this happen?" I like to think I have a good relationship with the big guy and try not to blame him for my woes. I did, however, say my prayers every night before I went to sleep. I tried not to sound too needy and understood he had bigger fish to fry, but if he had a spare couple of seconds, I could use some help.

- Guilt: You believe it's all your fault, maybe a lot of it is. I'm totally screwing up my kid's lives, and they will wind up in an orphanage. Try to take it easy on yourself. If most of the divorce is your fault, accept that fact and for God's sake learn from your mistakes. Guilt is like a 100-

pound weight strapped to your ankle. You have to get rid of it before you can move forward.

- Depression: This is all settling in now. The person I was supposed to of loved and he/she loved me back has betrayed me. I'm looking at Internet dating, bar scenes and whatever else single people do nowadays. You get to become friends with embarrassment, serious money problems and a host of other problems. Depression is inevitable during and after a divorce. Accept it and deal with it. It should dissipate with time. If you're having more depression than what you think you can handle, get some help! Or just get some help if you're just mildly depressed. Doctors, therapists, peer support groups and friends can be a big help.

- Acceptance: This really is happening to me. I have to devise some coping mechanisms and strategies to deal with all of this. There is no running away from it anymore. Time to face the music: I was already divorced in my head long before Sam filed. It would take a lot of time to accept all of this if I didn't want a divorce and didn't see it coming.

So you are divorced now. Grab an ore and jump in my canoe. Join the millions of other folks that have survived this life-changing event and me. *You are not alone*! I sincerely hope you and your kids will go on to a happy, healthy life together. Nothing is going to be exactly the same as when you were married. I know for some that is a bitter pill to swallow, but for others, it is a relief. It's time to build a new life with your kids and perhaps eventually with a partner.

I do like the metaphor of when one door closes another opens when it comes to divorce. I believe it is very appropriate. It is a new beginning; you will enjoy some of it and it will some take time to get used to some of it. There may also be parts of your new life that you will not find so enjoyable. Do whatever you have to do to get through the rough times. Peer support, therapy, friends, and healthy outlets. I have a friend that is a surgeon, and one of his biggest heartaches is that his patients complain that they are not exactly the same after a surgical procedure. He gently reminds them that it probably will never be the same. The same holds true in divorce and many times that is a good thing.

I know lots of divorced folks out there spend lots of time obsessing over who was to blame for their divorce after it is all over with. Does it really matter in the end? The end result is the end result, you are now divorced. Most likely nothing will change that. This can be a good time however to reflect on what led to the demise of your relationship, This is a great time to take a good long look in the mirror and take inventory of negative traits or habits. Do not turn this into you hating everything about yourself. Instead, look at it as an opportunity to improve yourself. You can also look into the same mirror and point out all the positive things about yourself. Just make sure you don't sabotage what could be a chance at a great future relationship by falling into some old bad habits or personality traits.

I still believe in marriage and think most of us are meant to be partnered with somebody. If you choose to stay single forever, wear that with pride. Just be happy with your life and who you are.

Welcome to the beginning of your journey as a single person. There will be bumps in the road, but you will make it! Don't be afraid to get help if you or your kids need it. Truly enjoy the good times, embrace and learn from the bad times and you will do more than just survive your divorce, you will thrive!

Final Thoughts

Thank you for buying my book; "Divorced Dad" Kids are forever Wives are not. I hope it gives you valuable insight into the divorce process and helps you through your divorce.

According to my attorney who has been practicing family law for over twenty years, my divorce was one of the most difficult he had ever dealt with. I felt this book could be a help to others going through the same event in their lives. This book is told to you from a male perspective, but I feel men and women alike would benefit from this book. I'm sure you found many similarities in your divorce after reading this book. I hope your divorce is not as bad as mine, though.

The most important element of any divorce should be your children. Do what's best for *them*! Your needs and wants are going to take a back seat to them. Use this opportunity (Yes I said opportunity. Turn it into an opportunity.) And let your divorce make you a better parent. You will probably not spend as much time with them as when you were married, so make the best of the time you do have with them. If you're not physically with them, take advantage of modern technology and stay in touch with texting, Face Time or whatever else is out there that will keep you connected. I try to make some kind of contact with my kids every day when they are not physically with me.

When you start dating, remember to put your children first. I suggest waiting, at least, six months before your kids meet anybody you're dating. When the person you're dating eventually meets your kids and they don't work out with them, it's time to move on. There can be no exceptions to this. Make sure the person you're dating is worthy of your kids.

Don't forget to take care of yourself during this extremely stressful time of your life. Try to gravitate towards healthy positive decisions and behaviors and stay away from the stuff that will not help you out in the long run. Keeping a good sense of humor during your divorce will be an immense help. Of course, there will be some very sobering times when humor will not be appropriate, but don't be all doom and gloom. I remember many times in my lawyer's office laughing out loud with him about Sam or her mother's antics. You would be amazed what a good belly laugh can do for you.

Spend the money and get yourself a great lawyer! Do your homework and make sure they are a good fit for your situation. Whatever the outcome of your divorce is, you and your kids will have to live with it for a very long time, and your lawyer will be a tremendous influence in this. Remember they are working for you. You are hiring them. Do not tolerate unethical behavior or be put in situations you may regret later by your lawyer. If this happens, get yourself another one. Do however listen to them. They are there to represent you. They should be experts in this area of law. You are probably not. Listen carefully to your lawyer, even if what they are saying isn't what you want to hear. They are not there to stroke your ego and make you feel good; they should be giving you a good healthy dose of reality.

Good luck to you and your kids during this journey forward in all of your lives.

I truly appreciate you taking the time to read my work. If you enjoyed this book, please consider leaving a favorable review wherever you bought this book. Also, if you could tell your friends and family about my books, I would truly appreciate it. Thank you. Feel free to drop me a line at www.kidsareforever@aol.com. I would love to hear from you. If you want to know the "whole story" of my divorce, check out the companion to this book, "Divorced Dad" Out of the darkness and into the light.

Made in the USA
Middletown, DE
21 January 2017